AWAKENING THE HARMONY WITHIN

How to Create with Spirit

Eugenia Oganova

AWAKENING THE HARMONY WITHIN

How to Create with

Spirit

Eugenia Oganova

ISBN -13: 978-0-9793817-1-3

For humanity's sake...

Contents

Living vs. Surviving

Living is a complex process, involving our material bodies, our energy fields, our consciousness and our link to Spirit. We are so used to surviving (which is a fight for existence), mistakenly considering that to be the very living we are here to do. But *truly living*, as a Soul in Matter, feels very different. While living in a true sense, a person is experiencing intensity of purpose, excitement, states of joy and harmony, while having a permanent link to a deep center of Self. There is a conscious resonance with the Higher Self and the Spirit of the Universe. One feels awake, alert, present and vibrant. The life force, or prana, runs through that person at a very high speed, constantly replenishing and regenerating all the body systems.

The state of survival feels very different. In survival a person is limited to worry, stress, competition and aging. Perception of life is filtered through the limited social views, perpetuating dependency on the social consciousness, while the access to the deep central place of Self is either limited, or non-existent.

At some point every person arrives to understanding that they are in survival and that they do not want to be in that state anymore. Questions like "there must be something more than this?!" and "what is my purpose, why am I here?" begin to surface. If you are one of these people, this book is for you. I endeavor to explain, in detail, conceptual systems which are <u>required</u> in order to move out of survival and onto living. I also describe, in detail, what the <u>practical steps</u> are that one can take to make this possible.

Personal Broadcast

No human being exists without a Light Body and an energy field. It is not possible, actually, to be an individual Soul without a Light Body. And it is impossible for a Soul to explore any reality in form without the energy field, including here on Earth, because it is the energy field that generates the physical body, not the other way around. In simple terms, the Light Body is a Soul component, a crystalline energy structure that holds our essence; the energy field is the oval shape bubble of multiple bodies of different frequency ranges, through which we feel, think, and know; all of these contain the matter-body, which is the material body we see. All of our bodies are composites of all of our experiences through all incarnations. The sum of these experiences is encoded as a unique personal resonance – a *vibrational signature* of individuality.

Each person is different, there is no such thing as "normal" here! The reason we all are different is because every Soul has had a unique journey through the Universe, through dimensions, through lifetimes. Even if two Souls were fascinated with the same idea, their experience of that idea would have been different,

3

generating different outcomes. So no one is ever "normal". In most dictionaries, normal is defined as common, average, ordinary, and unremarkable! What our human culture labels "normal" is simply the most common, usually the lowest passible, range of vibrations. In other words, the last thing you want to be is "normal"!

Our personality's uniqueness is based on the combination of genetic, environmental, and other lifetimes' influences. We incarnate into the genetic material that will support our awakening the most, we attract environments that will trigger our karma (unlearned lessons) and generate learning opportunities, and we experience life through the filters of other lives. All of that is for the purpose of focusing on the unlearned lessons and graduate to the next level of consciousness.

A person's vibrational signature can be harmonious or not. It is not a reflection of that person being "good" or "bad". The energy signature is evolving as it receives new information from new experiences, it can change in any moment. Our negative cyclical thoughts and emotions, negative pleasures and emotional toxicity of stress, even the type of food we feed our matter-bodies – all affect our Soul signature, and how harmonious it is, or not.

When someone is not living consciously, they are just existing. They have an energy signature, of course, but it is unrefined, and often disharmonious. Because the conscious awareness is low, that person might not even feel disharmonious. But as the Soul begins to stir inside, we start to notice the disharmony of our experiences.

This is the first step in awakening – noticing that what one has is imbalanced, and desiring something more than that.

Once there is a desire for harmony, we can begin cleansing the vibrations that are disharmonious. How do we do that? Every emotion, thought, belief, and food is a vibration. <u>Negativity is intent to stay separate from life, a denial of unity with Spirit, it is always linked to the desires and agendas of the Lower Self, the defended part of us</u>. So if we want to be more harmonious, we must clean up our inner messes: process stored emotions and let go of the negativity, change negative thinking patterns and challenge limiting beliefs, pay attention to how we take care of our matter-bodies, and the food we feed them. The more harmonious our outer environment is, the more harmonious the inner environment will be – choosing to create beauty and "high frequency uplift" will help our internal balancing. This also works in reverse – the more harmonious our inner world becomes, the more harmonious the outer life will be.

Negative thoughts and emotions need to be dealt with. If not, they are stored in one's energy field until one is ready to deal with them. But if we take too long, or keep depositing large amounts of negativity and stress that we refuse to process, we very quickly "fill up all the inner space." The result is the spill-over of these negative stored energies onto the matter-body. This is why our physical bodies get sick with chronic conditions. An acute physical condition can be a sign of processing, or facing an issue, and if we remain aware, it soon completes itself. Chronic conditions are the result of our refusal to deal with our mental and emotional baggage, so much so that it spilled over into matter. The behavior of incorrect eating habits and other improper ways of treating the matter-body are also a result of stored negative patterns in the energy bodies – emotional, mental, and others.

We are resonators. We broadcast our unique energy frequency, harmonious or not, and it attracts to us whatever matches it. This is the Law of this Universe that we live in – the law that states that "like attracts like". One of the definitions of "resonance" in a dictionary is "a quality of evoking response". If we carry a lot of fear, we will attract something that will activate that fear in order for us to have an opportunity to clear it inside of ourselves. A person with a lot of fear will attract to him/her people who are the *activators* of that fear (they trigger a fear response in us through their actions), and also people who are similarly afraid (they *amplify* our fear, making it very obvious). If we are joyous, we will attract more joy into our lives, and also the people who are joyous and bring us joy. This does not mean that everything in life will be pleasant, but someone with joy resonance will have more joy frequency even during a difficult lifetime, vs. someone who might have a fearful outlook and not a very complex life, and yet not have much joy in it.

This is not a punishment for having a "wrong vibration". We are the ones who created our vibratory signature and we are the ones who broadcast it. This means we can also change what we are broadcasting by changing who we are. If you do not like what your life is reflecting back at you, look inside for what are you broadcasting out into the world. Find the perpetrator thought, belief, emotion etc. and modify it until your life begins to match a higher, more harmonious, frequency. We are not victims of our circumstances – everything in our life is there because we have attracted it to us. We are the masters (in training) of our personal reality.

How do you know that you are supporting internal harmony and increasing your vibratory resonance? If your thoughts, words, and actions are for the highest benefit of you and all beings, you are. This automatically modifies the emotions you are experiencing and changes the circumstances you attract. It enhances the quality of your life. In other words, "take the higher road" no matter what, and your life will be of integrity and honor, attracting to you harmony and joy.

If we broadcast random signals (unconscious), we get messy life experiences. If we control our signals (mastery, consciousness), then we not only gain control *with* our life circumstances, but become more aware of the lessons. Taken further, we then can learn from these lessons, so we do not broadcast the same song over and over. And if we realign our broadcast to a more harmonious frequency, we gain control *with* the quality of our life experiences.

Let's look at this "control *over* life" vs. "control *with* life" difference. Even the mere fact of the existence of our biological form is a testament to the "cooperation programming", not the "survival of the fittest". Without cooperation and tolerance, our material body could not come into existence (it is a community of cells, all working together for the common good of the colony – the overall form), and neither could any human community (a culture could not develop without these principles). But even though the systems themselves were/are based on "cooperation programming", each individual consciousness had to learn this through inhabiting the automated systems (like a biological organism that is not self-aware) in order to become self-aware. And so as spiritual beings we do not live by the "survival of the fittest" programming. That way of living is based on the LOSS of consciousness – when the Spirit went into slumber as it descended into density. Self-awareness on the other hand is first discovered through the survival strategies, which allows that awareness to come into focus. This is what creates this "survival of the fittest" programming. It is not our spiritual code, but only a tool that we have acquired while inside density in order to transcend it. Once we begin to transcend density as our consciousness range expands, we let go of survival strategies as a way of life – which the "control over life" way of thinking is based on – and instead move onto the spiritual blueprint – which "control with life" is based on. In short, "control over life" implies a fear based existence of survival, and the need to control life in order to be safe; while "control with life" is about being a member of spiritual community, permeated by the life force, and it is about the *mastery of consciousness* instead of the override of life in order to feel safe. The "control with life" way implies internal safety as its foundation. Without internal safety mastery is not possible.

This is an amazing time to be alive on Earth. Our planet is changing her frequency range, refining higher vibratory patterns. This makes it possible for us to create the life we desire by altering our personal broadcast. The mess we have made of this planet so far is a reflection of limitation of "normal" consciousness. But masses (who define the norm) are made of individuals – and this is the time of individuality. The more each of us realizes that the planetary mess begins with each of us, the less mess we will collectively have.

Recognition of personal responsibility for our creations is the first step towards planetary harmony.

The universal flow is persistent, and it is intensifying. This shifts our planet into her next phase of consciousness. As this flow enters our humanity, it can intensify survival fears, emotional vulnerabilities, and powerlessness. Note that I did not say *create* these, but *intensify* them, because these issues were already there to begin with, and because awakening means "awakening to the traumas and shocks first, power later," not just power and pleasantries. Wrestling with these personal struggles is an act of courageous exploration into our internal unknown. We cannot become an awakened Self without the desire to *be* the Self. We cannot become aware and powerful without going through all of the powerlessness. To some extent powerlessness is necessary to show us what power is, because we learn through comparison in duality. It is naïve to assume that when we welcome the universal flow, we will suddenly leave behind all our troubles and "everything will be ok".

Truly free universal energy feels great, but when it first enters us, it hits all the blocks that we have, smashing them open. Don't you think that might be uncomfortable? It usually is an uncomfortable process, because we have to reevaluate our views on reality, and ideas and beliefs. But every time we feel the intensity of fear, and gain more tolerance to it, by processing the pain, we gain knowledge and experience, which eventually end in wisdom and power. And so with each block the clearing becomes easier, even if the blocks themselves are painful. This is the benefit for doing the processing work. The blocks are not necessarily any less traumatic or painful, but they do not scare us as much any longer, and do not define our reality, hence they are just uncomfortable. The wisdom is well worth it!

The time-space experience of Earth serves as a classroom in which we are able to focus our perspectives for the purpose of specific creation. The only reason for not creating what we desire, is because of remaining in a vibrational holding pattern that does not match the vibration of our desire. It matches the vibratory pattern of the block/fear instead! Identification of the discordant pattern/belief will quickly tell where we have "strayed" off the path of positive creation.

When we are harmonious, the Source energy (prana/universal ether) flows through us and creates.

It is the Spirit that creates through us, yet we are the ones who set the pattern for that creation! Through our perceptions we determine the preference, while the Universe provides the fuel and materials.

Once we are in such alignment, life feels exhilarating, exciting, passionate and fulfilling. From the non-physical realm of other dimensions you at some point had created a "denser you" – your material presence here on Earth. And once the "denser you" fully realizes its origin, and comes into the alignment with the Source of you, then the "denser you (material presence) can begin to truly create.

Desire

So much has been said about letting go of the desire as a means to awaken. This is not really correct. Desire is the fuel of the creation, and it is essential component of it.

We are the eternal entities who descended into this realm to experience the pleasure of navigating the Spirit, directing energy according to particular parameters of our material experience.

Desires are a natural outcome of our presence in the density of this dimension. We are in Separation. <u>Separation is a condition of perceptional limitation, when one's Self is perceived separate from the Source,</u> and from the rest of life. *We **are** everything even if our perception is focused on a detail of that everything* (i.e. a body and a Soul are not separate; your body and someone else's body, or any other object, are not separate; your Soul and other Souls are not separate; you and every detail of this Universe, in this or other dimensions, are not separate!) When we forget this, we see ourselves separate from others, and desire something we do not have.

We are constantly exposed to variety in everything. We live by investigating these options, tuning into them, trying them on emotionally and mentally. *Experience of variety while in perceived Separation generates preferences.* Desire to fulfill our preferences is a tool in constructing a unique Self – the very reason why we descend into density in the first place!

Variety → Investigation → Preference → Desire → Self

There is a big difference between higher and lower desire. Higher desire is in alignment with the Soul, it is for the higher good of all and the Self. Lower desire is only for the personal benefit of the person desiring.

When our desires are fulfilled it is not about the material circumstance, it is about the perception. We do not control others, ever. Every being on this planet has the right to experience whatever he or she wants. It is not up to us to determine what is ok to do and what is not. But it is up to us to determine what we want our own experience to be.

We do not control the behavior or experience of others, but we can control our own perception of events and, through it, our experience.

I often hear people's frustration with the diversity of desires on Earth. But merging all these diverse desires, perceptions and experiences into a homogenous one will defeat the purpose of being here! We did not come into this density in order to fix it. It is not our job to enlighten someone else, or to have them stop learning their way and begin to learn our way – no matter how harmonious we think our way is! Diversity stimulates preference, and everyone has the right to explore their way, no matter on what level of consciousness they are. The faster we accept that, the more fulfilling our own life will be, and the more success we will have in manifesting our own creations into material existence.

Manifestation of Desires

What is required in order to manifest desires?

- Self-identity in alignment with the Higher Self;
- Consistency;
- Allowance of the universal energy;
- Presence in the body for materialization.

Desire is not possible without the identity of Self, which is in itself a *focused intent*. Do not underestimate the value of your preferences, because it is they that shape the evolution of humanity.

Consistency of desire is required in order to manifest anything. How does one achieve consistency? Three components: remain focused on the desire, feel the final result "without the proof of fact", and eliminate doubt by the means of Mind mastery (*more details on this in "Mind Mastery" chapter, page 127*).

Whatever it is we focus on and feel – we create. This is a very important distinction though, not just "whatever you mentally focus on", but *"whatever you focus on and feel"*. If you have an issue with something, a fear, you must work with it, i.e. you will have to think about it and find the beliefs that generated it in order to transmute it (more about it in the later chapters) – and that is ok. But when we focus on something feelingly and remain with that focus, we create it. Witnessing feelings with our minds, parallel to experiencing them feelingly, is beneficial to our development. Experiencing feelings without any mental Witness is detrimental to our spiritual growth, because we become limited by the perceptory range of that feeling (*in my book "Mission Alpha" I explain the concept of an Inner Witness in more detail*).

Worrying is using your imagination to create something you do not want. The vibration of your being immediately reflects the vibration of what you are tuning into emotionally.

Exploring mentally is ok, it is a personal <u>investigation</u> and it allows you to <u>challenge old beliefs</u> and create new ones. Judgment of your feelings, beliefs or actions is not "mental", it is an *emotional reaction*. And that emotional reaction is the denser point of focus – whatever you emotionally focus on is what then is downloaded into your "creator matrix" as an input for "desired creation".

Judgment and worry link us to the opposite of what we want to create – we are afraid that "it won't happen", or that "something bad would happen." Judgment and worry become a "reverberated pattern." We focus on the negative emotion that reflects the negative thought (opposite of what we were thinking to create), only to reflect the belief that it was based on, and now we are focusing on that negative belief – instead of what we wanted to create in the first place! We are focusing on the Saboteur instead of the Creator! (*I explain more about dealing with that Saboteur in "Intentions and Manifestation" chapter, page 137*). The more you are focusing on that "reverberated pattern" (the Saboteur), the more you think in it, the more you vibrate like it – which means the more stuff/people/events that vibrate like it are attracted to you. This is how we create our own hell, the personal version of our own fear (fully sanctioned by our own homebred Saboteur). This type of energy attraction will continue indefinitely, until you offer some other broadcast, some other vibration. And when this different vibration is offered, life will match it instead of the old broadcast. But changing of the vibration is totally up to you. Every single one of us is in control of this procedure, each one of us has the power to do it.

Everything in our lives is there because we have invited it. We did so through our own emotions and thoughts, through our beliefs. Nothing can ever occur in our experience, material or otherwise, without our personal invitation. And so when you are aware of what you are feeling and thinking, you are in position to exercise *absolute control with* your own experience here on Earth in a matter-body.

Why are we, Souls, doing this? Because we are taking our mind patterns, beliefs and thoughts, further than they have ever extended before, we are creating something new – the Self. The confusion and worry one experiences is easily replaced with clarity and power once the understanding is achieved – that we are vibrational beings, creating through our broadcasts.

One of the best pieces of advice that my guides had given me when I was wondering if I could make my desire come into manifestation was: *"Find a way, or make one!"* This is essential to our understanding of Self. We tend to think that if someone else (especially a lot of people, the majority) do not think something is possible, it means it is not possible. That is NOT true! As William Cowper said: "Absence of proof is not proof of absence." Sometimes the map for what we want already exists and all we need is to look for it. That might be a very complex difficult search, but what we want is there.

Occasionally there is no map. If your desire is pure (i.e. comes from your Soul/Higher Self, not your Ego) and you know clearly what you want (your Ego is consciously aware of the Soul's desire and is in agreement with it), and no matter what happens to push you from that path, you still want it, then this is where you must do your own research and experimentation, until you MAKE your own map.

Become satisfied with what you have and what you are. Yet at the same time, yearn for more. Without hindrance of unworthiness, doubt, and other limitations stand at the edge of what is coming, but meet it with cheerful anticipation, not impatience.

For example, let's say you want a piece of chocolate cake, badly. You do not have any in your house; it is an evening and it is pouring rain outside – dark and windy. But you still want the cake and so you brave the weather and drive to the store. While you are driving, you realize that the weather is much worse than what you had thought. At this point you have two options: you can choose to keep going and get to the store where the cake is, or you can turn around and go home, choosing to spend the night cake-less, and then buy the cake tomorrow. But no matter what the weather is, you do not start wondering if the cake even exists!

Yet this is what we tend to do. We notice our desire, we go for it, then halfway through realize that it will either be more difficult

16

to achieve than we initially thought, or that we will have to wait a little for it to happen, and we turn around! Some people spend their entire lives going back and forth between the origin point of desire and the midway point where they have encountered an issue, and eventually collapse of exhaustion.

The only reason one experiences something one does not want is because one is giving more attention to what one does not want.

You are the creator of your experience. The circumstances are only perceived as "factual" by our limited brains – the third-dimensional linear time materialistic perception that allows us to grow and learn about ourselves. If you run into a wall, this does not mean that it is an insurmountable obstacle. This is simply a component of your learning. Perhaps you can climb over the wall or dig under it, or there might be a hidden door. Perhaps it only appears to be a wall because of your current perception?

Responsibility for Our Creations

The past and the future only exist from our perspective. In universal perception everything is. It is always in the Now. Here in the material world we have to plan, strategize, learn from our past. So "being in the now" does not negate learning from the past or planning. Instead, it is about the change of perception – to look at life from that expanded perspective of the Soul, outside of linear time.

Every belief that has ever been constructed still exists. Every thought that has ever been thought still exists. Why? Because everything *is*. A belief is a program, each developmental stage of which is like a photograph frozen in time. A thought is a vibration. What makes us have an emotional response to a thought or belief is our focus.

By paying intense attention to something we come into an alignment with it. The more time spent focused on a thought, the larger groove it will carve in your mind.

Whenever you focus on a particular thought (your own or someone else's) you reactivate the vibration of that thought inside yourself.

This is why when we are surrounded by the people and experiences that match what we desire, it is easier to maintain the personal experience that we want – we simply resonate with the others. This way one does not have to have mastery in upholding a particular frequency, it is being resonated by one's environment. And it is much harder to maintain an experience (by generating particular thoughts and emotions) if it does not match the external state. For example, if one is experiencing dis-ease, and desires to enter the state of harmony where the body is healthy, it is hard to maintain this clarity of thought/belief if others around are convinced that one will only go downhill from there.

And so we must gain mastery with the issues that generate negative thoughts in order to transmute them, while consciously navigating towards more harmonious frequencies.

For example, maybe you used to feel victimized by life but for a long time now you feel confident and on track. Then something happens which makes you feel bad, and that feeling is the one you had when you used to think of yourself as a victim. If you allow this feeling to flow, while you breathe through it, and you choose to focus on higher beliefs, like "I know this situation looks similar to the ones I have been in before when I felt victimized, but I know better now, I am the creator of my life and I choose to look at this situation as a learning experience" – then you *transmute* the uncomfortable feeling. Lesson learned. If, on the other hand, after you have felt that unsettling feeling you choose to focus on "feeling bad", you will immediately run into the thought that you have been victimized, linked to belief in injustice and powerlessness. Instead of transmuting the feeling it will grow, fed by your focus, and reactivate the previously held beliefs/thoughts of yourself as a victim that you used to have in the past.

We all have experienced this at some point – you think you are "done with" something, and then one trigger occurs and suddenly you feel bad all over again, even though for a long time you were able to not fall into that pit. This is because by focusing we amplify. And everything that has ever been experienced is still out there, in some other "now", and we can experience it again by focusing on it. As Abraham, the collective intelligence channeled by Esther Hicks, says:

The only way to deactivate a thought is to activate another.

This does not mean that we abandon self-investigation – that is the only way to uproot and deal with the inner Saboteur of our desires. But in internal research the feelings must only be used as *sign posts*, as indicators of which thought pattern/belief we were in when that feeling occurred. Sometimes it is very difficult to find the belief, but it is always easy to find the feelings. If one does not possess elaborate comprehension of one's feelings, one can learn by focusing on them – by deepening into a feeling. This will allow a person to differentiate not only the "good feeling" vs. "bad feeling", but also the nuances. Once the "emotional vocabulary" is established, every focus on feeling will produce a deep emotional charge, so at that point it is not necessary anymore to focus on the feelings, only to *recognize* them, and link them to the internal belief programs.

If you can imagine it, you can make it happen – but the small print is "as long as your desire is in alignment with the Divine Plan".

If one desires to "change the world" or even to "change the world for the better", this essentially means that one wants to impose one's idea of "better" onto the rest of the world. Since every sincere desire is granted, one probably will be able to generate a strong matter-based idea and even a following of others who might agree. But the end result will still be learning that this was not a harmonious creation.

When one is in alignment with the Higher Self, the creation is achieved through personal (internal and external) effort, and is fueled by the Spirit. When one is not in alignment with the higher components of oneself, there is no support from the Spirit for that creation, even though the material for the creation is still available – this is why disharmonious desires are able to materialize, but they require more personal effort, more pushing, and in the end they take the person further into Separation, not closer to Source.

There is such a concept as *habitual vibratory pattern*. This is one's base note for attraction and resonating. Your habitual vibratory pattern represents the grooves you have carved inside your mind – your most commonly held attitudes, most often visited beliefs, most habitual feelings.

Practiced attention to one's attitude results in an overall higher personal vibratory note. By raising our habitual vibratory pattern, we develop stronger protracted proclivities for Harmony.

Sometimes the person who is doing the desiring (i.e. the creating) is so involved in the trauma, which they are in at that time, that it is impossible for them to *receive* what they are creating! But if the desire was in alignment with the Soul/Higher Self of the desiree, the benefit is still occurring, but it is received either by the people who are in the same timeline, but are not in trauma (i.e. they are allowing), or by the future generations.

Our ability to desire is a component of the Soul's quality – curiosity. We are eternal Soul entities and when we desire something, we focus all of the power of our Soul entity in one point. True, harmonious with the Higher Self, desires are very intense, they consume our being because in that moment we can feel the power of the entire entity funneled into the point that is us. Yet there is no *longing*, for that implies separation from what we desire. Instead there is *yearning,* an excited anticipation, an expectation of the conscious *experience* of what we desire (which implies connection with it in the first place!)

Who Am I?

Every person at some point in their spiritual awakening arrives at the question *"What am I supposed to do in this life?"* At that point we are awake enough that we want to be more than our current limited perceptions, but we are still bound by the concept of "supposed to". No one out there determines what you are supposed to be! You are "supposed" to be YOU. That is just that. So the more proper question here would be *"Who am I?"* And discovering that answer is a life-long process...

We are never a "finished product". The Universe/God is not perfect, it is in a State of Becoming Perfect.

There is no such thing as a "finished Self" because the term finished implies a final goal. But Spirit has no goals and no finality! When we solidify in our beliefs and perceptions in an attempt to become the perfection, we are not any longer moldable by Spirit. Each of us is an ever-changing Self, an entity, evolving towards more and more harmony.

So, who are you? The answer to this question is a combination of three parts:

1- Personal Uniqueness (What are my unique Soul qualities and lessons which I came to work with?)
2- Discernment of the path (Am I going in the "right direction?")
3- Acceptance of uniqueness of others (Am I avoiding my lessons by judging others' behaviors and beliefs?)

1: How do you recognize your unique Soul qualities and lessons? Your Soul qualities are the vibratory patterns acquired through many lifetimes. Some are <u>beneficial for your being (conducive to spiritual growth)</u> – these are your talents – and others are <u>non-beneficial (karmic detours)</u> – these are your unresolved issues and misconceptions about the nature of this Universe. We create life lessons to resolve these non-beneficial patterns, and we use the beneficial Soul qualities to help us. Your beneficial Soul quality might be your innate ability to listen, or to see patterns in math, or dance. People often envision their Soul quality as something extreme – like being able to speak some other language without studying it, or to play an instrument amazingly well. It is true that these do exist, but they are rare. And they are simply more obvious, not "better"! One Soul quality is never better than another, they are all unique and perfectly suited for the life that person is living.

You might wish you had the talent to play piano, for example, as some famous child of five years of age is doing, because everyone admires him, and you think him to be "special" – i.e. "more lovable" than you. But you do not know the life circumstances of that child. It is very possible that the reason that entity chose to bring this particular Soul quality into his life, is so it activates the lessons of perfectionism, pride, or loneliness, or dependency, even victimhood.

In other words, love the life you are in. Love the Soul qualities you have – because they are perfectly suited for your particular life lessons. We often take our Soul qualities for granted because they seem too natural to us, too easy. Some people are natural mediators, others are natural warriors, some are natural deep experiencers, others are natural doers, or natural supporters, or natural investigators, and so on.

2: How do you know you are "going in the right direction"? Well, first of all, there is no ultimate "right direction" – there cannot be, since we all are unique. Second, there are clues about the direction of your unfolding which can help you understand if it is harmonious with your Soul or not.

For example, if you are experiencing joy, which is a Soul quality, you are on the Soul path. But remember, joy is different than satisfaction or comfort, these are more likely your Ego's experiences than the Soul's.

Soul is who you are as an entity, and your Soul is in the "state of becoming" – IT IS:

Soul = Is-ness of you, the eternal you.

Soul and your Higher Self are connected. The Higher Self is the part of your personality that translates Soul qualities into useful personality abilities. It is the wise part of you.

The Ego is your "operating personality", the part of you that interacts with the world, that *plans* and then judges itself and life depending on if external and internal expectations were met or not. Ego is the part of us that feels satisfaction if it gets what it wants. Ego can courageously step ahead if it is allied with the Higher Self, or it can be incapacitated by negative beliefs when it is allied with the Lower Self.

The Lower Self is your defense mechanism. It is the part of you that carries fear, anger, and pain-based reactions to life as a means of protecting you from more pain. It forms when we are little children, and we experience pain (physical, emotional, mental, and spiritual). In attempts to prevent this pain from occurring again, we generate beliefs that promote behaviors we perceive will prevent pain from happening again. The problem is that these beliefs are composed by a child-self, they are reactory and not based on Higher Self truth. Lower Self can be loved and supported, so that inner hurt can be processed and let go of, instead of festering and generating more defenses. But when Lower Self and Ego ally, we get just that. And so what was a child's strategy to avoid a parents' anger becomes an adult's strategy for survival in life.

The discernment of your feelings and emotions is essential in being able to understand if what you are experiencing is a true Higher Self guidance in harmony with your Soul, or if it is simply an Ego, and perhaps Lower Self, satisfaction.

It is also important to pay attention, if you are noticing the intensity of emotion, desire, or passion associated with the direction you want to take. You have to be very honest with yourself here. Excitement or satisfaction, or general happiness about doing something, can very easily be assumed to be generated by the Higher Self, yet be the experience of your Ego instead.

But there are few things in life that will elicit this incredible Higher Self intensity – these are the moments when you touch your Soul. It can be when you picked up a book to read and your whole body is vibrating as if this is one of the most important decisions of your life to read this book, and everything that will come out of that will be significant. Or it can be a moment in a conversation when you know you must speak the truth, even if you never have done that before, and your whole being is resonating with the intensity of the words that come out of you. Or it can be the extreme experience of freedom that you feel after some decision is behind you – may that be your conscious choice, like to get divorced, or to have a baby, or subconscious choice, like being laid off from a job.

3: How do you know you are not respecting the uniqueness of others? It depends on what kind of judgment, positive or negative, you apply to life. Positive judgment is essentially discernment, an ability to differentiate (which is obviously necessary for sanity!) Negative judgment is really a glorified personal opinion.

If you are judging others' behaviors or beliefs, it implies that you are believing in "ultimate right" and "ultimate wrong". Out of that assumption comes the conclusion that if you are right (and your feelings tell you that you are) – this means others, who believe differently, have to be wrong. Or if they are right, then you are wrong. This is the basis of all negative judgment – we emotionally defend our position, forgetting that we have the right to an opinion without having to prove anything! Because all of us are unique, we all will have different beliefs, and feelings and actions that come out of them. Our responsibility is to pay attention to our reactions to other people's expression of themselves. Our reaction carries in it an unlearned lesson – we are reacting because our own conviction is not as stable as we would like it to be, and we perceive external stimuli as a challenge, or as an activator of pain. The pain was already in us, the wobble was already hidden in our belief – but if we do not take responsibility for that (and extract the wisdom from our reaction), we project it outside of ourselves, perpetuating negative judgment.

Self Design

Much effort goes into designing our existence in matter before each incarnation. Souls review and craft in detail all aspects of their lives in matter. This pre-incarnational set up of curiosities, desires (and fears, too) pushes through the Self point into the physical incarnation. The designed Self is made of many components of the total identity, the type and arrangement of which makes us unique. These pre-set components include:

- Body physicality – health, particular predispositions (encodements) for dis-ease, ethnic characteristics, height, activity/passivity needs, big-boned/small-boned, cellular/nerve sensitivity, food preferences and needs;

- Geographical birthplace and timing, which places on earth are the power activation points for this particular person, which places relate to particular difficult karma or previous joyful experiences;

- Relationships – family, lovers, children, friends, co-workers, enemies – who carries what for us: support in learning, an activation of karma, loving trust;

- Desires, hopes and dreams – these influence perception and life choices, the means of releasing the karmic baggage, and also components of Soul curiosity to learn something new;

- Psychological attributes – emotional, mental and spiritual tendencies, both fear-based and joy-based, as needed for the incarnational goal.

All of the desires, drives, characteristics and impulses that are encoded into us are there to guide us. They are the Soul's strategy for each lifetime. And the key to that strategy is Self-Identity, it's a requirement.

All are recorded in a <u>Soul Contract – the purpose of that lifetime, the incarnational goal (finishing what we had started and stimulation into a new creation).</u>

One of the easiest ways to begin self-investigation (the search for the Soul Contract within us), is through conscious self-experience. First you have to align with your Higher Self, so when you are doing self-investigating, you are tuning into yourself feelingly not from the Ego or the Lower Self parts of you, but from the Higher Self, or the Ego in alignment with the Higher Self. Do you particularly like something about yourself – your height, your hair, the tone of your skin or eyes? If so, this is the component that is meant to support you – so look at how that feature has helped you so far. Did it make interacting with some people easier? Did it create a resonance with someone who had helped you?

Is there something in your material presentation that has caused you particular anguish over the years? If so, that is the key to your "lesson plan". What do you like about your personality and what don't you like? Are these qualities mirrors of your parents' personalities, or are they totally "alien" to your family? If what you like about yourself you have learned by emulating your parents, these qualities are your "gifts" – they are the reason your Soul chose this particular family to incarnate into, or be raised by. If what you do not like about yourself is copied from your parents – these qualities are components of your karma, something you must process through, understand and transcend. For example, if you incarnated into a family where one or both parents were confident, even fearless, you might also feel confident in your own abilities to face life's circumstances – that is a "gift." Or if your parents had money fears which resulted either in scarcity mentality or hording, you might copy this belief and as a result have financial issues – this is a karmic overlay to work on (if it wasn't, your Soul would have never chosen to incarnate into this family in the first place). The "alien" to your family qualities can also be karmic overlays to work through, but most often they are your "gifts", what your Soul had given you as a "magic tool" for the time when you would need it. Either way, karmic overlay or a "gift", these qualities of your personality need to be investigated, paid attention to. If they seem negative to you – study them. For example, if your whole family is logical and responsible, and you are a "free spirit" who cannot figure out what to do in life – this simply showcases that you are a fluid magnetic personality and must advance in the use of that side of yourself. Or if you are sensitive and insightful, but your family is rigid and society-based, they might judge you, but you have that sensitivity for a reason, it is something that you needed for your awakening this lifetime, and being born into a family where you would stand out by contrast is only meant to enhance your trust in your own sensitivity and insight.

Our problems start not when we encounter uncomfortable experiences, but when we get stuck in them.

Prior to incarnation we set up certain challenges as part of our journey here. These challenges then act like magnets, which attract situations to us, so we can experience them, resolve them, and learn and grow the Soul Self through them. The Soul's unique "signature" is the energy pattern woven from these awakenings. If one resists the challenging situation, which arrived into one's life, one becomes entangled in it – and attracts negativity that matches the problem, instead of the Light/Code (*more on that in "Is-ness and Illusions" chapter, page 93*) that matches the solution.

We resist our lessons by:

- Believing the literal meaning of the events – trying to solve the situation, rather than to learn about life;

- Allowing the emotional response to the event to take over – that is the "fluid overwhelm", the over-focusing on the emotion, too much energy in the Emotional and Astral bodies, not enough in the Mental and Conceptual bodies (*you can read in detail about the anatomy of the human energy field and all these bodies in my book "Mission Alpha," in the 1st Chapter)*;

- Freezing up – hiding from emotion, avoiding it, attempting to stoically not feel;

- Pushing against the event by becoming frustrated or angry – that is an attempt to create distance from the event, a separation of Self and its' creation;

- Judging and blaming others – a victim mentality of "It's all their fault! I had nothing to do with it! It happened to me!"

- Judging and blaming self – a collapse response of "It's all my fault! I can't do anything right!"

When one's *not-wanting*-to-experience what one *is* experiencing becomes habitual, one grows stuck in the resistance. Any and all resistance is futile – it only leads to more pain.

Learning to recognize the signs of this habitual stuck-ness releases Ego's literal perception of the event, and instead amplifies Soul's metaphorical perception. Ego's literal view is mostly processed through the body's autonomic nervous system, which is unconscious, instantaneous and preconditioned. The Soul's metaphorical view is processed through the body's central nervous system, which is comprised of the spinal column and the brain, and this allows for more of the Soul's expanded awareness to enter our material experience. Because we habitually take the Ego's side, we respond to problems as trauma, instead of problems as teachers.

An example of these two views can be a situation where one has flu symptoms – sneezing, coughing, stuffy nose and overall feeling miserable. The literal Ego's view is: "I must have gotten this virus from someone, it invaded my body and generated all this mucus, I need to go to the doctor, I need drugs, or I won't be able to function well, and this is not acceptable!" The metaphorical Soul's view is different: "I was so sad last week, but did not give myself space to process this sadness and grief over my disagreement with a friend. This weakened my boundary, making it harder for my immune system, I must need more water element to be in kindness and love as I process this sadness and grief energy so I release the anger and do not judge myself or my friend, I need to make space for myself to regenerate my boundary."

Since each human being has a physical presence inside this third-dimensional environment, each human is a component of the Divine Plan – the communal design/Experiment by all of the Souls involved in learning on Earth. If you are alive, happy or not, you are needed by the Solar System, or you would not have been given permission to have a matter-vehicle on Earth. We all are necessary pieces of one complex puzzle.

Each human being has the *right* to exist on this planet. But we need to decide if we *want* to exist, and the power of this desire comes from the Fire Element.

Fire Element is one of the essences that compose life as we know it, along with Water, Air and Earth Elements. These essences are conscious and they can be referred to as "Elementals", the beings from the energy of which we create reality. There are more Elementals in the Universe than these four, but for our development on Earth we must first master these four. Each of the Elements represents particular types of energy/qualities. In simple terms, Fire relates to desire and passion, Water to love and connectedness, Air to clarity and inspiration, Earth to support and comfort (*I explain the Elements in much more detail in my book "Mission Alpha", 5th Chapter*).

If the passion of the Fire Element burns inside of us, then the intense desire to be alive, and the commitment to that existence, becomes anchored in space-time, and we claim our unique expression. Not being anchored in space-time sets up many problems for the physical body. The body consciousness has difficultly locating itself in time and space, which generates fear and feelings of danger, these feed the Lower Self, which in turn sabotages the Soul strategy for that lifetime. Obviously our mental body can look around and know which year it is and what place on Earth we are located at in this very moment. But the body is a complex computer-like system, and it registers all of the lifetimes that the Soul has experienced. If we do not want to be in this body (we judge it) and do not want to be at the location we are in materially, the body might feel that it is operating from another lifetime frame. The body-computer would scan the other lifetimes and pick something else to relate to, which relates to the feelings we are having. When the body attempts to energetically straddle the past and the future, parallel to the present, it generates severe emotional and mental difficulties for us.

We can reactivate this desire to exist, the inner Fire, by first recognizing the issue, then rebalancing it:

- Lack of Fire feels like "being not good enough", fear of "getting in trouble", "nobody cares about me", feelings of despair, "I am not wanted, I only get used by others". It is refusal to anchor the focal point of Self, hiding from life, a form of minimizing one's presence in the world.

- Overabundance of Fire feels like rage at life for not doing what we want it to do, entitlement, arrogance, pushy-ness, denial and the lack of patience. This is also a refusal to anchor the focal point of Self, but in the opposite direction – taking too much space and not letting anyone else exist, it is an exaggeration of one's presence in the world.

Both of these imbalances come from rejection of one's Soul Contract. In this avoidance we do not want to be who we are, instead we want to be someone else – in a different body, with a different personality, different talents, in a different location, and so on.

We have designed ourselves perfectly for this lifetime. This does not mean that we are "perfect beings in every way", obviously not – there is always room for growth, for improvement, for learning and transforming, which is the whole point of coming into this existence. But *we are perfect for this lifetime*. Dealing with the dissatisfaction and jealousy about not being something else we think we should be is actually a way of comprehending who we are, to fully claim that focal point of Self. This is the rebalancing of the Fire Element that brings us into a perfect state of *desiring to be the Self that we are*.

The balance with this Fire Element desire energy often is missed due to the <u>absence of comfort</u>. Human beings became addicted to "feeling good" over the thousands of years of being unconscious and animalistic, and so we continue to be driven by this "feeling good" instead of by what is beneficial to us. When we follow the path that is in our Soul Contract, it is not always "feeling good" because entering new territories requires discomfort, and we are trained to see discomfort as "bad/not feeling good". <u>Courage is definitely required in order to live the</u>

life we have designed, and true comfort does not come from always "feeling good", but from the experience of *preciousness of life* (Self included). We all are wired to be open to the universal energies, clear in our perceptions, well-boundaried and personally unique. It might look very different from person to person, but we all, in a harmonious state, have these abilities. By claiming personal space (the right to exist as you) one desires more to exist as an individual, which amplifies the experience of preciousness. As one confidently makes that boundary and courageously takes the space for oneself, the inner focal point of the Self is reached. One experiences one's own preciousness in this Universe.

The Matter-Body

Think of yourself as a person, sitting in front of a computer. You want to play a complex computer game. You do not feel (with your emotional body) the zero-one-zero-one-zero-one programming of the software, and you did not design (with your own Conceptual body) the hardware of the computer machine in front of you. But you want to play a game, you have a desire to fulfill. What do you have to do in order to perceive *inside* the computer game? You must make an "avatar", a character inside the game. Your avatar will have a form/body with which it will be able to perceive the game environment as its reality. The avatar will know nothing of you, the person in front of the computer, who commands it, right? The avatar is your eyes and ears inside the game, through it you can *experience* the game as if you are in it, even though you are sitting in front of your computer. Now, let us look at what this avatar can do. Can it do anything, have unlimited options? No, of course not, the avatar has to act according to the rules of the game it is created for. In other words you, the person in front of the computer, can move left, right and so on, but your

36

avatar must move only according to the rules of the game. If you want your avatar to open a door and go through it, you command it to do so, but it can only do so according to the game rules – maybe it will have to turn around twice, or have to have some special key, or maybe it will have to do some task to gain access to the key, with which it can open the door you want it to open.

In this analogy, the person in front of the computer is the Soul. The higher desires and thoughts that person has are the interaction with the game, they compose the Higher Self. The avatar, designed to perceive the game from the inside, is the physical body. Through the senses of our matter-bodies we see, hear, smell, taste, and kinesthetically sense our material "game" here. The avatar is "experiencing" the game by translating the stimuli – these are our lower emotions and thoughts, which make up the Ego. The avatar is also defending against perceived or previously experienced pain – this is the Lower Self. But just as the avatar is not the actual consciousness, our physical bodies, complete with their reactions to stimuli, are only perceptual tools for the Soul.

The word "energy" comes from Greek "*energeia*", which means "within" and "work/activity". The matter-body is enlivened by the "work within", or energy. In fact, it *is* energy. Every atom is more than 99% empty space! The subatomic particles are really energy bundles, the compressed coded vibrating packages of information. They seem solid to the "avatar" that we, Soul entities, perceive through, because it was designed to play by the rules of the game – the matter game (what is labeled the laws of physics). You, the Soul, know very well that matter is an extremely slowed down energy. Nothing is solid. It only feels solid because we believe it is. We all communally agreed on the rules of the matter-game, and one of the main rules is the limitation of matter (i.e. the avatar should not be able to walk through a wall, it will have to look for a door, find the key, and only then enter). But in reality, it is not solid. Just like the walls of the house inside a computer program are made of programming code, not brick or wood!

When we incarnate, we enter, by choice, "the game" of material perception. In order to have a matter-body respond to our commands, we affect it with energy from other bodies (Emotional, Mental, etc. – *read more detailed explanation of the energy field anatomy and all the bodies in my book "Mission Alpha," 1ˢᵗ Chapter*). Inside the material body, signals travel through the DNA and RNA to generate and maintain our cellular structure. The intelligence that encodes the particularities of the matter-body is us, the Soul. The intelligence on which it is all based and out of which it is all made, is the universal energy (*a more precise explanation of this is in the "Energy, Prana, Ethers" chapter, page 49*).

Self-Determined Safety

Until one begins to do one's personal work of awakening, there is often very little understanding of how much fear one carries within. Most people, if you ask them "do you feel fear?" will tell you an adamant "no!" That is because socially it has become more appropriate to acknowledge an experience of anger, or disappointment, or worry – but not fear. Yet all these expressions are secondary to the initial fear that activates them. Only when we begin to dig inside our perceptions, deepening our experiences, do we understand how much fear we really have! That is good news! Once the fear is recognized and not shunned and avoided, it can be cleared.

The term "danger" usually means impending possibility of injury or death. What we perceive as "danger" is an ending of a
38

particular state of being which we are fond of. For example, survival danger is when circumstances are threatening to destroy the "avatar" – either render it incapable of receiving and processing the stimuli of the "game", or effectively terminating our material presence altogether (severely harm us or kill us). When we are in eminent physical danger, the animal part of us goes into survival mode. Your body can react faster than your mind in these circumstances – because it is *designed* for the material "game" of life, and will do what it can to preserve the "avatar". But experiencing a physical illness, even the life-threatening kind, is not danger – it is a lesson, yet we tend to add our fears to the experience as if it were, perpetuating the illness instead of healing it. This is because we see it from the "avatar's" view point, not the Souls. Soul knows no danger.

There are different levels of not feeling safe – from physical danger to emotional or mental ones, even spiritual. These are imbalances of our perception, not actually dangers (danger is a made up concept). How can we be in danger if our lives are "classrooms" for our learning? Learning can be difficult and even painful, but it is our erroneous perceptions of Separation that turn it into an experience of "danger."

When we see ourselves as powerless, or separate from life we can experience circumstances outside and inside the physical body as danger. This does not mean we are really in danger – we experience danger in relationship to stimuli which makes us believe we really are in danger (and for the Soul there is no such a thing!)

Physical illness, for example, is a message, something we can learn through and not only heal the body itself, but also enrich our consciousness in the process. Yet if an intense fear arises when the body is unwell, it is based on these three misconceptions:

1- Forgetting that we are the Soul inside this body, the body is only a perceptual vehicle, and so with or without it we have continuity of consciousness. This misconception is a fear of death – funny how it can arise even during a common cold!

2- Forgetting that we are conscious co-creators with our material vehicle, that we can have a relationship with it and help it heal – the body already has all the blueprints it can possibly need to repair itself, it is our fear that gets in the way. This is about not trusting the body's intelligence – we tend to assume that someone else, like a doctor for example, can know more about our body than we do. It is always helpful to remember that although doctors can be very useful, you are still the only expert on yourself, you have spent a much longer time with your body than your doctor ever will, and you know it more intimately – so be open to suggestions, but in the end it is you who makes the decisions, not the doctor.

3- Forgetting that no matter what negative stimuli we have encountered, we were the ones, who placed it there, on our own path! When it seems that "bad things just happen," and we "catch a virus" and are "victims of accidents," we let go of our highest power – free will choice – and instead become victims of circumstances. This misconception is about not seeing yourself as a creator of your physical situation.

If we work with these three malfunctions in understanding when we are sick, for example, or experiencing some sort of physical difficulty, we can help our body to get well sooner.

The next time your body is sending you a message:

1- Notice the survival fear arising inside you, honor that fear – it is the truth on your Emotional level at the time you are experiencing it. But do not give it a further story like "oh, I'm going to die!" or "Oh, there is something really wrong with me! I have to fix it right now!" Instead take a deep breath downwards, then further into the Earth. Do this a few times until you feel calmer, then bring the energy upwards, from the ground, all the way to your head – this helps to remind you that you are a Soul inside this body, not only the body.

2- Remind yourself that you have created this body for yourself. Utilizing the genetic material of your parents you modified it to fit your life's journey this time around, and so your body is perfect for you, it has all the mechanisms to heal itself. Tell your body "I trust you, I will help you heal yourself, and I know you can." (Even if you do not fully believe it, repeating this several times will help).

3- Stay connected to your body – you might still feel the fear, but "take the higher road", the Higher Self view point that _you are safe because you chose to be_. Safety is not based on the environment (internal or external), it is self-determined. If you believe yourself to be safe, you are. So ask yourself "What is the message here? What is my body telling me?" Have curiosity about the message so that you can heal and at the same time enrich your consciousness.

Understanding the lesson resolves the physical issue and it has no more reason to exist.

When we focus with curiosity on the lesson, instead of spinning in fear, we "get out of the way" and the natural healing abilities of the body can do their job. In other words, if we worry and are fearful, we stop body's ability to regenerate, but if we are curious of what we are learning through the physical imbalance, we not only help the body heal, we also become more awake.

If one focuses on "not being in danger" or on "protecting oneself", one is only amplifying the perception of danger.

When we attempt to be safe by focusing on protecting ourselves, we actually end up feeding our fears! Remember that your focus is what you amplify within, broadcast outwards, and then attract.

Focusing on danger will, in turn, attract circumstances of danger as an opportunity to clear the initial misconception. The idea of danger is based in Separation.

As soon as one resonates with the connectedness of all life and expands Self-perception to incorporate the Soul, there is only safety and harmony in diversity. This effectively ends the state of Separation.

So in conclusion, if in the moment of physical pain or other difficulty you can honor your fear, but focus with curiosity and kindness on the lesson – you bring the energy back into your own center. That is the Self determined safety.

Victim "Virus"

Inside the animal kingdom in the wild there are no victims. An antelope is not a victim of a cheetah that hunted it, and the young bear who lost a contest for domination to an older bear is also not a victim. Their self-preservation instinct is simply the material form's programming to preserve the "avatar," or its young, when possible. When not possible, the animal Soul "leaves the game", and the body dies. By the programming of instinct animals know with absolute certainty that "all is as it should be". This same understanding is all-permeating once human beings arrive to a higher level of consciousness – we know that everything that occurs happens because it has attracted the participants together for the learning, and eventually there is no cruelty and other separation-type learning. But the intermediate phase between the animal consciousness and a more enlightened human consciousness is a very chaotic step, filled with misconceptions about personal value and power, and their opposites, victimhood and powerlessness.

Victimhood is a denial of one's power.

As a transitional step, experiencing the victim state is a way of recognizing that one is out of alignment with one's Soul Self (the Divine Self). But once one becomes addicted to the absence of responsibility that is inside of that victim perception, the victimhood perception of life becomes a habitual pattern. Worst of all, this pattern tends to be self-replicating, like a virus it spreads through one's system if left unchecked.

The experience of projecting responsibility onto something external "feels good", because it is easier than being responsible and dealing with one's broadcast. This victim infection limits one's ability to connect with the Higher Self and Soul, which keeps one stuck in that victim mode. This no-power-state impacts the energy field, which further limits one's ability to process incoming data, which makes one *believe* the experience of the victim mode due to the perceptual limitation.

Every human being on the planet has victim patterns to heal – some from the current lifetime, others from the karmic overlays of other lives. Here are a few very obvious ways to recognize when one is in victim mode:

- irritability, which is dissatisfaction with reality – victim of circumstances;
- doubt, which is about not being sure about one's power – victim of fear;

- confusion, which is simply a refusal to deal, to face life – victim of overwhelm;
- hatred, which is a desire to erase something from existence – victim of competition;
- rage, which is desire to harm – victim of entrapment;
- worthlessness, which is a self-denial and collapse – victim of pain.

Energy, Prana, Ethers

Energy powers all Creation throughout this Universe. That Energy has been called Oneness, Nature, Divine Intelligence, "unification energy," prana, ether, and many other names.

This is how "everything is one" – even though we are each individual with a unique consciousness, we are all sharing in the Energy that sustains each cell, our beings, the whole Universe inside and around us.

Energy is everything – energy can be twisted and programmed whichever way, becoming anything. Like a material chair, a negative thought, a positive emotion, an entity in another dimension – all are energy.

Prana, or *Life Force,* is "pure energy", the energy that has not been modified into anything yet – a "neutral energy." Prana interpenetrates and supports everything in this and other dimensions. A material rock was originally prana, but now it is a rock, i.e. a densified energy pattern.

Ether is the etheric component of prana/life force, the lowest, densest prana inside every dimension. The etheric level is the first level of every dimension and of our energy field, the "body double" of our material body. Ether is the type of prana, a neutral energy, which is the closest to matter.

To summarize, Energy is the totality of Creation, prana is that Energy in an undifferentiated form, and Ether is the slowest, densest component of prana. The word "ether" comes from Greek, where it meant "the upper/pure air" – it is seen as "above" from the inside of the density of matter. All life is supported by Ether – our material bodies, animals, plants, Nature, even what we consider an empty space.

Think of it as this: what we label "solid matter" is an extremely slowed down energy. In other places where we do not see solid matter, there still is the same energy, but with faster speeds. What is an empty space from the "avatar's" perception might be a very active territory from the Soul's view point!

Our bodies are made of slowed down energy. Our emotions are made of slightly faster energy, this is why we do not see them physically. Our thoughts are even faster energy, so are our deep feelings, our love, our beliefs and ideas. All of it is energy. The matter-body is a composition of atoms, held together, activated through chemical reactions, united into cells – all holding inside themselves volumes of information from the Etheric body, fueled by Ether.

48

The Etheric Body is a blueprint for the physical body with all of its organs and cellular systems. It is filled with micro-circuitry and it is bright blue in color. The etheric body anchors safety, stability, vitality and physical health. It is a blue, scintillating "spider-man" suit surrounding and interpenetrating the physical form, around every cell and organ, transmitting the information that the physical body uses to manifest itself. We wake up in the morning, every day, and perceive our bodies, pretty much, as they were the day before. They seem to age because we have a program in the Etheric Body that follows the dictate that all life forms age. The more awareness that we have of the Etheric Body, the more we can become sculptors in body-clay, allowing our forms to take on new shape and become more alive.

There are four types of Ether available to feed our Etheric bodies. All ethers exist in the color shades of blue, the densest ones being bright blue and the lightest ones being pale blue. They also differ in "texture"/substance.

- *Chemical ether* (this ether is the "densest" form of food for the Etheric body, it is a planetary-Nature ether, responsible for the atomic, molecular and cellular integrity of forms); when you tune into your *existence* in form, you are tuning into this ether;

- *Life ether* (a somewhat less dense planetary-Nature reproductive ether, it is a force to "continue existence", responsible for cellular colonies coming together, cooperating and maintaining forms; when you tune into *harmony* in the body, all small "parts" functioning well together, you are tuning into this ether;

- *Light ether* (Solar-Nature ether, which is much lighter, and is a means of receiving information about "creation into form", a view of the form as an entire directional process (seed-plant-fruit-seed) and access to the information (senses like smell, taste, feeling, hearing, seeing) through sensations, colors, and vibratory patterns; when you tune into the *cycles* of your body, cycles of life, you are tuning into this ether;

- *Reflective ether* (Moon-Nature ether, the lightest almost-transparent one, it is responsible for the reflection of Nature – a sort of temporary copy of creation for the purpose of its growth, it carries the sequences of creation of planetary forms (DNA of entire species, options for modifications already attempted); when you tune into *options for healing, options for harmony, extinct species, planetary memory files*, you are tuning into this ether.

It is useful to develop conscious relationships with these Ethers in order to gain Mastery in matter. Study yourself – which Ether do you feel most connected to? Which one is the easiest to feel? Which one is hardest? Work with the less familiar Ethers, and notice the changes in your body.

Color and Ether

Light is made up of photons, each one having its own energy and hence its own frequency. The frequency range of the electromagnetic spectrum that is visible to the human eye (and which we refer to as "color") is a very small region of the entire range of the photonic spectrum of Universal Light. Our physical eyes only see what we label as "physical reality." Some of our machines can translate/see radiation, microwaves and radio waves within their parameters. The sixth chakra, or third eye, can perceive other colors though the pineal gland translation, which are outside of the range of physical reality. We would require "consciousness vision" in order to see other dimensional entities,

50

structures of higher consciousness, and even our own energy bodies.

The sub-atomic particles which constitute matter (protons, neutrons, electrons) are bound together in atoms, molecules, crystals etc. Any "collision" may be enough to excite oscillations in these bound structures. An atom can be "excited" in different ways: collision of energetic particles with atoms, collision between atoms, thermal chemical reactions, collision with invading photons etc. These frequencies of oscillations are measurable and calculable through quantum mechanics and "solid state" physics.

Once these particles have been excited, they immediately seek to return to the lower energy states from which they came. This is accomplished by the *emission of photons*.

The electric field of an electron ("orbiting" the nucleus) is directed to the nucleus. When an electron oscillates due to the "excited" atomic state, its electric field becomes parallel to the oscillation and the magnetic field becomes perpendicular to the oscillation. This oscillation of the electron creates a transversely-oscillating magnetic field, which is radiated away from the nucleus with the velocity of light. And so *the emitted photon is released at a 90 degree angle to the oscillating electron.*

Our matter-perception is based on this 90 degree weave of oscillating electrons and photons - it is the Code for this perceptional "simulation" we call Material Reality.

A complicated object will have many possible oscillation frequencies and hence will emit light over a wide range of frequencies. Substances tend to emit in certain regions of the electromagnetic spectrum, including frequencies we can see as "color." The physical matter (color in a particular shape) that we see is only a small portion of what "holds matter in form." For example, in organic matter chlorophyll tends to emit in the green frequency range – that is why plants look green; and anthocyanin emits in the red frequency, that is why tomatoes are red.

Colors as frequencies have particular effecta on human energy systems and so using colors consciously is yet another tool on the journey of Self discovery.

- For strength/vitality, resonate with the color Red.
- For pleasure/creative juice, resonate with the color Orange.
- For clarity, resonate with the color Yellow.
- For non-judgment/unconditional love, resonate with the color Green.
- For truth, resonate with the color Blue.
- For insight/higher vision, resonate with the color Indigo.
- For wholeness/unity, resonate with the color White.
- For rest/calm/peace, resonate with the color Black.

What does it mean to "resonate with color"? Well, definitely not just "think about this color". <u>Resonance with a color is an experiential perception of color frequency</u>. Imagine yourself *becoming* that color, use all your senses – not just the visual one – what would this color feel like, smell like, sound like, etc.

At the sub-atomic level "color" is not an intrinsic property, because this level is directly supported by pure life-ether: the same electron is just as capable of emitting X-rays, orange light, or radio waves. At the sub-atomic level, within the nucleus of an atom, the difference between energy levels is substantially greater than the differences that typically occur between the electron orbits around the nucleus. And so when transitions occur within the nucleus, the spectral lines are at much higher frequencies so that they do not fall within the visible "color" spectrum that we can see with our eyes. Thus color is a property of complex substances (molecules, crystals etc.), rather than of the constituents that make them up.

Each life form is manifested into existence by the Ethers of the Etheric Blueprint – the Code that programs its Etheric Body. Within this program there are interactions of constituents, all of which generate visual effects that we can see.

What makes colors is the environment and interactions the electrons find themselves in contact with, i.e. what Etheric Blueprint they belong to, or which interaction is supported by that blueprint of the Nature Grid. On other words, we create our reality by affecting atomic oscillations, generating "what we need to see" inside this perceptional "simulation."

Color could be explained as a sound frequency recorded visually. Bright colors generate refreshing and potentizing rhythms inside of the human etheric body. Bright colors can act as energizers, and even anti-depressants, for an etheric body when it is low of charge.

By focusing on color we are teaching our material bodies to metabolize Ether.

Whatever is considered sacred is defined as "connected with God". Energy/prana/Ether is sacred. By learning to perceive and use it, we dismantle energy addictions to "false sacreds" (like money, body image, food, status, ego achievement, etc.) and become more alive. Energy/prana/Ether is truly the Fountain of Immortality! In the future humanity will be able to live by metabolizing Energy/prana/Ether only, not requiring any consumption of physical proteins and other constituents, because the body will be able to generate anything it needs, being linked with the universal Energy flow.

Sacred Geometry of Light/Word/Code

Sacred geometry is a "configurative language" composed of Elemental imprints and the divine creative force (the masculine and feminine aspects of Spirit) that has birthed all of life. Sacred geometry is literally a direct conduit to prime consciousness, to Source. It is a short-cut through the dogmatic and limiting beliefs (of human unconscious generation), leading directly to the transpersonal knowledge of Unity.

The term "Light" is often used in the awakening teachings, and most people who are just beginning their path into consciousness tend to mistake the meaning of it as a dualistic component, as in "Light" vs. "Dark."

54

The primary infrastructure of all existence is Spirit – unrealized and realized consciousness, explored through Light/Word/Code, and bound together by the resonance of Unity/Love.

The term "Spirit Light/Word/Code" as I am using it here is interchangeable with the terms: "Spirit's Light", "Codes of Light", "Music", "Harmony", "God's Word", "Logos", and the "Code of Creation" – it is the Light that is beyond duality, it is the Word or the Code that created/programmed this Universe. Inside that Spirit Light/Word/Code are contained dualistic components of Light and Dark, positive and negative. In this dualistic understanding, the Light is what is "seen", the conscious, and the Dark is what is "unseen", the unconscious. One can also look at this dualistic pair as Light being the Mind and structural, the yang, while Dark being the feelings and fluid, the yin. The non-dualistic Light/Word/Code is an "illumination", which contains duality.

When we commune with sacred geometric forms we interact with fields of informational influence – the design Codes of the Universe, constructed of Unity/Love. It is the language that precedes, and transcends, all language.

Geometric forms are not just abstract random shapes, they are conscious units of creation, alive in their individualized awareness. A sphere or a triangle is a rudimentary consciousness, while the dodecahedron, or the star-tetrahedron, is a more complex consciousness – all different types of "Code of Creation"/Spirit Light/Word.

When Sacred Symbols were first used by the human beings on earth, the goal was to concentrate the mind on the Spirit/the Infinite One and particular components of the Light/Word/Code. A symbol is a powerful conceptual tool used for focusing multitudes of disjointed perceptions into one. Symbology is a method of keeping the eyes (physical eyes and/or the third eye) focused on the symbol, so that no outside interference (sights or sounds) distract from the higher concept.

Unfortunately when we begin using the symbols, we are only able to perceive their consciousness within the range of our own perception. And so many people tend to worship the symbols (anything from a picture to an idol). In doing so, they project their personal authority onto the symbol, which only leads to feelings of powerlessness and dependency.

As one progresses on the path of awakening, the symbols become repositories for intention. Similar to storing our intent in a crystal, we can also align our intent with the meaning of the symbol. The larger the group of people who does this, the more charge and influence a symbol will have, because people build a morphogenic field around it (*more about these in "Morphogenic fields" chapter, page 159*). An example of such compounded intent on a symbol can be an icon, a statue, or a carving of a geometric symbol that is considered alive – not because people believe that it in itself *is* the "god", but because they feel it as a *conduit* to God/Spirit.

The more enlightened one becomes, the less need there is for any material representations (like statues) and the geometric symbols themselves are chosen instead. A symbol then becomes a picture for focusing on the energy pattern it represents, and serves as a means to keep the mind from wandering. As a person enters an understanding that there is only one Spirit expressing itself through the Light/Word/Code – the Unity Blueprint for this Universe – then various geometric symbols are seen as attributes related to nature, to health and strength, to social well-being, to perceptional range – in other words, to the whole welfare of humanity. This stage of awakening effectively ends worship and sacrifice of any kind. It is understood that no part is above any other part or has to be sacrificed for the good of the whole, as all parts are equally necessary.

From the beginning of human development, three symbols were consciously used by all human cultures – the Square, the Circle, and the Equilateral Triangle. The reason for this is because these three symbols are the Codes of Spirit for human development, representing primary steps on the journey.

__Square__ represents the Earth, and with it – Balance. It stands for the "Four Corners of the Earth" as four cardinal directions, and for the "Four Pillars" (the Elemental forces of Fire, Air, Earth and Water) which created order out of chaos, and now uphold existence. Currently human kind attempts to use the "Four Pillars" to suit its selfish desires, this is the awkward and pain filled-learning stage that will eventually result in the balance of a realized Self. The Square is about equality, mastering it allows one to move beyond the duality of good/bad, male/female, within/without.

Circle represents the Source/Infinite Spirit, purity of potential wisdom, unconscious harmony, infinity (everlasting). Circle's Code is that a Soul, as a part of the Source/Spirit, always was and always will be (even though it will change). This is a symbol for integration of all aspects of our being. It is linked to harmonious experience of life, Self, and others, knowing that all is interconnected and that we are the resonators and co-creators of our experience. Wholeness results from alignment with our Higher Self, after releasing all that no longer serves us.

Triangle represents Inner Guidance and the Trinity of Creation (*detailed explanation of this Trinity is in "Is-ness and Illusions" chapter, page 93*) It is the "breath of life" as we allow the opening of our transpersonal nature. The triangle empowers, because this pure energy movement enhances the Integration and Balance of all aspects of Self.

When these three symbols are fully understood, they are compounded and others added, generating complexity and eventually leading to Enlightment.

Each symbol is an entire concept, an aspect of the Light/Word/Code. Communication with the symbols is yet another tool one can use to harmonize and raise one's vibration. You can utilize your feelings, intuition, thoughts, or visual and auditory sensory responses as you relate to one of the symbols. Hold it in your mind, envision resonating with it, or imagine taking it into your body. What does the symbol offer you? Building a relationship with the symbol is a conduit to the energy pattern that the symbol represents.

Enlightment

Lately that word, enlightment, has been used in multitudes of spiritual New Age literature. Hindu writings provide their understanding of enlightment, and so do many esoteric books. But what is the enlightment that spiritual students so keenly seek?

I can tell you that it is usually not at all what they think it is! Most people's idea of enlightment, firstly, is based on an assumption that they will be above lower energies when they are enlightened. That is a misconception, generated by the desire of separation from negativity and seeking some sort of "spiritual utopia".

Enlightment is the state of conscious connectedness to all, the opposite of separation.

We do not become enlightened so we can escape lower vibrations. The entire idea is silly, considering we came here to experience these lower vibrations in order to become enlightened!

The second idea about enlightment is that it is a neutral state –
a state of complete detachment from life to the point of zero. That
is also incorrect. The peace, if not a zero, neither is it neutral.

Peace is an undefended interaction with vibrant life of any kind, sometimes all at once, while knowing that you are not limited by it.

The third common view on enlightenment is that it is a superior
state to the one we are in. It is not. There is nothing ever superior
to anything else, it all just IS. We go through losing our god-like
understanding during the periods of involution into matter realities,
and then we regain, and improve upon, our god-like understanding
of ourselves during the periods of evolution into enlightenment. One
is not better than the other. No one decided to punish us by sticking
us down here into matter, so that now we have to grow out of our
inferiority, and learn to be enlightened. The Spirit/Source learns by
deepening into the density of unconscious potential and
illuminating it with understanding.

So what is this enlightenment? Enlightenment for an atom might be
very different than enlightenment for a plant, and even more different
than enlightenment for a human being. There are stages to
enlightenment – more and more harmonious existence. To get to this
harmony we have to go through the disharmony, it is a necessary
step. For us humans, an enlightenment is a state of harmony inside
our system to such an extent, that it allows the highest parts of us
without restriction to communicate with the lowest parts of us. We
have a physical body and the lower four energy bodies – Etheric,
Emotional, Mental, and Astral. In a full enlightenment state we also

have higher energy bodies – Truth, Unconditional, Conceptual, Time, Crystalline, Support, Memory, and Unity. In the current stage of human development, we have a physical body and only seven energy bodies: Etheric, Emotional, Mental, Astral, Truth, Unconditional, and Conceptual. Even though these bodies exist in us as a species, most human beings consciously function only in the lower three energy bodies, and even that is usually without much freedom. Some explore the fourth, the Astral, and usually are unaware of the Truth, Unconditional and Conceptual components. The bodies beyond the Conceptual are not yet formed in most human beings. From this perspective, an enlightment is to go through a stage of discord of the Astral in order to become fully aware of the higher three bodies, Truth, Unconditional and Conceptual, and harmonize the lower with the higher. This will deliver us to a stage of enlightenment. But it is only a step. The next step would be to go through yet another disharmonious period of exploration to construct and incorporate the bodies beyond these seven.

When we begin to do personal internal work, we courageously look at our issues, take personal responsibility for our reactions and pains, process the stuck emotions and release our dependency on others. We are meant to be self-sufficient entities, but our matter-bodies believe that we are dependent on others. When we lost/forgot our higher understanding of this game, the "avatars" became the Self. In other words, the body's perception of dependency, caution and need to protect in order to survive was transferred onto the other energy bodies, inculcating the attitude of survival/protection in our psyche. We forgot the freedom of independence.

Our "avatars", the human bodies, are "born naked" – we do not have claws, fangs, fur cover, sharp scales, we are not capable of fast speeds, our limbs and jaws are not extremely strong... Our only means of remaining alive is the use of mind (which can result in logical cooperation with others), caution and seclusion. The body learned to use these means to survive, and we learned to believe that this is necessary. It is only necessary from the standpoint of the "avatar", from the matter-body view. These protective mechanisms, instincts, helped our species survive for thousands of years in matter.

When we do internal personal work, we remind ourselves that we are more than our "avatar". We begin to feel less dependent on the external world – on opinions of others, on our own judgments, on status, money, family, career, "experts" that supposedly know better about us than we do. All this work cleanses our lower four energy bodies, helping them to work in unison. This is a stage of discord on its way to inner harmony – it can be very difficult to dig through these issues.

When the lower four bodies work in unison, our sensitivity increases, and we begin to experience the rest of ourselves – our higher energy bodies. We notice that our Truth body can tell us if something is true for us or not by having a harmonious or disharmonious resonance. We experience states of non-judgment, even if for short period of time – these are related to unconditional love and joy of connectedness. We begin to become aware that our beliefs are conceptual programs which can be modified and expanded, clarified and enhanced, until their influence generates the result that we desire. Our concepts generate particular thoughts, which then generate feelings, emotions, and actions, which further affect the external world, attracting or repelling circumstances, people, and things.

We did not "fall from an enlightened state" into this density. We came from a harmonious state of being into density, but we did not have the conscious Self (inside this Universe) to experience it as individuals. Enlightment implies individuality, a balance of unique Self and Unity.

An enlightment is a synchronization resonance of the lower four energy bodies not only among each other, but also with the higher energy bodies.

This is when we feel content. Everything clicks into place, we are acutely alive in Higher Truth and Higher Knowing.

This resonance allows the enlightened
Soul-Self
(the "I AM" of the Spirit)
to be activated in us,
as the energy of Light/Word/Code
of Divine Intelligence
resonates through all our energy bodies
simultaneously.

Our Divine Rights

All of these issues we come to earth to work out – karma, family, genetics… Do we have any rights?? Yes, we do. We each have the rights (under Universal Law) to be a unique Self, the right to exist, the right to desire, the right to personal truth. There are many more rights that we do have as incarnate entities. But often the messages we receive from people are exactly the opposite. We are taught that saying what you actually feel is inconsiderate, or that wanting something will only hurt you. Or even that being yourself is rude. We are told we will hurt other people if we name the truth, that it is impolite. When one claims the space for oneself, or considers one's needs first, then one is seen as selfish or arrogant. We often hear that we will never know or see the spiritual world, or God, because it is too far out of our reach. But we all have the right to our spiritual Self!

A human being has an energy field and inside this field are the chakras, or energy vortices – they are the doorways through which the energy is attracted into the body and flushed out of the body. In a harmonious individual, chakras are open and the energy spirals into them. In a disharmonious person chakras can be clogged, or even closed. When the Energy/prana/Ether is absorbed through the chakras, it then is distributed along the vertical tube channel for the whole field, through the "Caduceus of Hermes" to the nervous, circulatory and endocrine systems (in the Vedas these channels are called Pingala and Ida "nadi", which coil around the central Sushumna/Merudanda), and through the meridians (which are used in acupuncture) to organs.

In a harmonious human being there are seven main chakra pairs (front and back vortices) and many minor chakras (on the hands and feet, at the liver, etc.) Above the head there are five
64

more transpersonal chakras which link us to the Soul-Self (the "I Am" of Spirit).

Each of the main seven chakras is responsible for a particular energy frequency, which also coincides with a divine right.

The vertical tube (the central energy channel of our bodies) holds the right to be unique. When the energy flows freely through the vertical tube, we are able to stand in our personal uniqueness.

Two vertical chakras:

The root chakra reflects our divine right to exist – if you are in a body, you have the right to be here, period. One's Soul Contract with the planet is one's "legal documentation" for one's right to be here in matter.

The crown chakra is the right to know. This is not a mental knowing through analytical thinking. Crown chakra knowing is conceptual and holographic – it is a deep understanding, when one's whole being is involved, not only one's mental capacity. And we have the *right* to know what we *need* to know.

Front chakras:

The second chakra is the right to like or dislike something. You might not have an option of not doing something, but you still have the right to not like it. The ability to like and dislike is a requirement for creation!

The third chakra is the right to want. This is not the same as "having it" – you might not have the right to have something (for example, it is not integrous to steal), but you always have the right to want it anyway :) It is healthy to want, otherwise we lose the desire to create.

The <u>fourth chakra</u> is the right to be undefended. Believe it or not, we were not designed to walk around in all this "armor" of fears, anxieties and paranoid hyper-vigilance. We have a divine right to be open. This, of course, does not mean "be exposed" as in "naked". We still need to have a healthy boundary to define ourselves, but without the "armor".

The <u>fifth chakra</u> is the right to speak our truth. If we speak our truth of the moment with kindness, it allows change. Speaking the truth in order to hurt is not the same as the divine truth expression. Truth is not meant to be a weapon – instead it is a transformer, anchorer and opener.

The <u>sixth chakra</u> is the right to see reality inside the illusion. When we get stuck on the circumstantial story, we forfeit our divine right to see with clarity.

Back Chakras:

The <u>second chakra on the back</u> is the right to have energy for our awakening through the participation in what we need and want. The saying "when you get older, you have less energy" is a lie! We have the RIGHT to have all the energy we want/need for our lives. But we have to believe it, we have to claim it, we have to let go of limiting beliefs about illness and aging (they only serve our fears).

The <u>third chakra on the back</u> is our right to be whole. We are meant to be harmonious and in resonance with life.

The <u>fourth chakra on the back</u> is our right to choose – it is the free will. People often live their whole lives in reaction to external circumstances, not realizing that they gave up their right to freedom, all the while feeling trapped. Don't let that be you. Circumstances are only the triggers for the issues we already have on the inside. Dealing with these issues directly allows you to exercise your free will.

The fifth chakra on the back is the right to be independent. But it comes with the price of self responsibility. If you are fully responsible for your Self, then you become independent.

The sixth chakra on the back is the right to strategize. If you have one idea after the other, but can't seem to figure out how to make them come into material reality, you are not using your right to strategize. It is one of your divine rights, which means that you are capable of figuring out anything you need to figure out! Any idea that you come up with, or fully align with, you can generate a materialization strategy for.

Believing Without Proof

The physical body cannot tell the difference between a strong emotional experience based on an imagined/visualized (non-physically perceived) event, and an actual material event. To the body's perception they are the same – both real.

The Higher Mind/Soul-Self, can infuse our higher energy bodies with the Divine Intelligence of Light/Word/Code, which then influence our mental body, which further affects our emotions, which then affect the matter-body. In other words, our physical and emotional bodies serve the mental body, which receives messages from the higher bodies.

This means we program our matter-body, quite literally, from wherever the internal alignment reaches. If we are harmonious and conscious, the alignment is between the body and all the other bodies, all the way to the Soul resonance itself – then the Soul's influence reaches all the way down. But if we are confused and are inside our emotional and mental struggles, then the alignment from the physical body only reaches to the mental body – and its mess is what programs the physical body! This is how we create disease and pain. In order to create a new state of physical balance, a state of ease instead of dis-ease, we must have clarity and vision, harmony inside our energy system.

How do we create what we want? Well, the result will depend on which part of us wants it, right? If your desire is pure, i.e. you have a curiosity about an experience and chose to enter that experience in order to *comprehend* your Self – that would be a Higher Self's, and Soul's, curiosity/desire. Or if you want to have something because you are afraid of not having it, i.e. you have fear about lack and you want to have an experience to *compensate* for that lack – that would be a Lower Self's, and sometimes Ego's, desire.

We create from the strongest charge (the most potent broadcasting frequency). If you have a pure curiosity/desire, you now can work with making it happen (which we will talk more about in the next paragraphs). But if you have a Lower Self or Ego desire, instead of manifesting what you think you want, you will attract what you are afraid of. Why? Because the fear was the driving mechanism for that desire, the fear was the stronger frequency. Consequently, it makes sense to check your desires first – and if you find that some of them are based on fear, change them. Otherwise you will only be programming "avoidance of pain" through fear…

For example, a woman is seriously ill and she has a desire to not have that experience. If she is afraid of the repercussions of her illness and wants to get better, to "not be ill", she is in negative desire because it is based on the fear and avoidance of difficulty she is facing. On the other hand, if she knows that her illness is a lesson and her job is to learn something about who she is through that lesson, then she can have a desire to learn, and to experience a state of health. Instead of "I don't want to be sick anymore" it becomes "I choose to experience a state of health, to experience healing as I am learning about myself through the process".

In order to then create what we want, we have to have the correct internal state of mind programming.

First we have to look at where did our programming come from? We come into this life with some of it already, we are pre-programmed by the Soul. As we have looked at it before, some of it is learned lessons, or wisdom, the rest is the unlearned lessons, or karma. Because of these programs we chose the appropriate environments to activate the lessons. This is why we pick a particular family, with particular life circumstances for the beginning of a lifetime. We receive secondary programming from the genetics of the matter-body we entered into. Then we acquire more programming from the social structure – first of our upbringing family, then from the peers and other social connections (school, church, job, etc.)

The sum of these programs is what makes up our personalities, our fears, desires, our reactions to stimuli. Anything we create in our internal world, and our external lives, follows the internal programming. If you do not like how you feel – find the program that generates this feeling and change it. If you do not like something that keeps showing up in your external life, find the program that it is based on and change it.

We are meant to be Creators. But in order to create consciously, we have to become conscious first – otherwise our creations are echoes of our pains and fears (because these pains and fears are louder broadcasts than happiness and harmony).

When we are clear and in alignment, we see the world as it is – beyond the limitations of matter-perception.

An ability to envision, to see, to interact with other-than-matter components of this life - this is prerequisite of creation. Your abilities to envision are the "training wheels" for your Godhood.

We are meant to create worlds, environments filled with characters to play in them, forms we, as consciousness, can enter and explore, just like we created this simulation we call material life, and the "avatars" we call our bodies. Why do children visualize so much stuff that is "not real"? It is real enough to them! And it is because they, newly entered into this matter world, have an echo of memory that they are Souls/gods, therefore they keep attempting to create whatever world they want – they imagine it into existence! To us a child running around the room with a stick in his hand and a pillow between his legs is just that – the boy, the stick, the pillow. But he is riding a dragon, with his sword drawn, into the unknown – and his matter-body believes it because he, in that moment, believes his creation. Or a girl wrapped up in a curtain is just that, the girl, the curtain – but she is a princess in a castle, and she can see it all in every beautiful detail, and her body believes her…

Interacting with energy guides, angelic entities, yours and others' Higher Selves – all of these require your faith in something outside of this matter-based world. If you want to be able to change the programming of your system, you have to first *believe* that there is more to your system than the matter-body, then believe that your consciousness can *envision* a different you, and that you can *become* that new you.

Why do we lose the ability to believe other-than-matter reality? There are three most common reasons:

1- We do not consider non-physical stuff "real";
2- We are afraid to be deceived;
3- We are afraid of the unknown.

Even people who say that they "believe in energy" (I have always found that funny – energy *is*, no matter if you believe in it or not), believe in guides, energy beings and so on, they still struggle to actually interact with the non-physical world. I often hear "I want to see my guides, but I don't", "Why don't I hear my guides?", "I have been intending for something every day, and yet nothing has happened..."

The first reason – non-physical stuff as "unreal": What is socially acceptable we consider to be real, and what is not – to be unreal.

The "real" is simply a communally agreed upon reality, a limitation imposed onto the consciousness range by agreement with the perception of the masses.

In olden times, for example, having a vision was considered real, and it was assumed that it came from God. If you told someone today that you have visions, they might think that you are psychotic with delusional tendencies…

The point is that whatever we experience is REAL to us. If you see/sense/feel a being's presence next to you – that is a truth for you. If you started with a guided visualization of, for example, entering a cavern, but then the vision took off on its own, expanding into something you saw – that is real. If you had a vivid dream and felt some extreme emotion in relationship to it – it is real. But it *means different things* – that is where the wisdom is! Most people are scared of vivid dreams, especially if they seem to be about something negative (like that your friend dies, or that you find out something you don't want to), and then either dismiss the dream as "stupid" (this is avoidance of true reality), or take the dream literally (as in, if someone dies in the dream, this means they will die in material life). Neither is true! The *emotion* is the truth, not the story! The emotion you felt in the dream is the message – something you are already feeling in your subconscious but for some reason do not want your conscious mind to see, it is coming out to be noticed. It is not a *prediction* of how things will go, it is simply a message about what already *is* in your subconscious. Vivid dreams are not predictions, but messages about what *is* that we did not notice…

If someone told you that nothing that you see is real – it would be hard to believe, right? That is because you rely on the body senses, and the *body* tells you that what it can touch, smell, taste, hear, and sense is real. But if you remember that it is the body's senses, and that *you are not the body*, it stands to reason that you must have some other senses beyond the physical to perceive "the rest of" reality, right? The act of allowing that concept to exist in

72

your system already means that you can receive information from other than the physical body's senses.

In other words, in order to perceive non-physical reality, one must first accept a belief that one's *identity* is not of the matter-body, but of something else.

The second reason – Fear of being deceived: We are often ridiculed as "weak" and "gullible" if we allow ourselves to be played on, tricked. It is a social standard that states that if you were tricked, this meant that you were an idiot to begin with, a weakling. And being one is bad/shameful, and also very much painful because then others laugh at you, take advantage of you, or push you out. With all this baggage it is very hard to have faith!

There is a reason why we cannot have the proof before we believe it to exist – it is because we cannot attract what we cannot resonate as!

We have to believe first, the proof comes later because we generated the vibrational beacon able to attract the frequencies of what we believed in – hence the proof!

The third reason – Fear of the unknown: It is based on the fear of not being in control.

Why do we care to be in control? Because we are still under an assumption that we can avoid pain!

We get hurt, we do not want to repeat that pain and so we come up with this idea that if we "did everything right", or if we were in control, we could prevent the pain and in doing so be better off. Pain is a teacher, just like everything else is, thus avoiding it only creates suffering. We can have moments of acute pain when we are in disharmony, but if we attempt to avoid that experience, we fixate on the pain, not harmony. This grows the potency of the pain frequency. If we are not careful, we make this focus habitual, which makes the experience of pain chronic.

Chronic pain is suffering, and suffering is not necessary, ever! But acute pain experiences are part of our learning.

Also, when we wish to be in control, we imply "mental control", which relates to the Ego. In other words, we want our Egos to be in control. How can we enter the world of non-matter realities if we want the Ego, which is a matter-based composite, to be in control? It's like saying "I want my body to be in control of the experience of music" – it is illogical. You might perceive music through one of the body's senses, hearing, but that hearing is only the means to experience, it is in control of maybe clarity or loudness of sound, but not of the actual music. Same with non-matter perceptions – your Higher Mind (from the Higher Self and the Soul) could be in control (*see chapter "Higher Mind", page 83*), but your Ego could not, it is only a component of the experience, not the driver.

Imagination / Visualization

Imagination is very different from fantasy. Imagination is expanding into possibilities (and visualization is a way of doing it visually), while fantasy is arranging these possibilities into a story. When we imagine something, we open up and allow information we receive (visual or otherwise) to arrange itself into a pattern – which then brings the "aha!" moment because it "feels right". In other words, by the use of imagination we expand to match existent but not yet available to us energy patterns. Imagination initially has a degree of goal directedness – i.e. whatever is our focus that would be the area we will expand into. Thus, if someone is focusing on the harmonious frequencies, they will expand through imagination into these possibilities/patterns. But it's equally possible to focus on the disharmonious energies and expand into them through the use of imagination.

Fantasy on the other hand is a personal free-flowing arrangement of these perceived frequencies. We expand and we perceive the possibilities which were not available to us through the material body's senses (that is imagination so far), but then we arrange these images into a story that we come up with based on what we already know (instead of allowing the information to arrange itself) – that is fantasy.

For example, a child is tuning into the possibility of something non-physical being present in the room with him (this is neutral). He is using his non-physical senses and he bumps into something

75

he cannot place, a feeling, sensation, maybe a smell, which is an indicator of something being in the room with him. At this point, if his focus is on the harmonious vibrations, his perceptions will arrange themselves into something he can comprehend – a positive helpful feeling, a friend in the room. This is still his imagination – an open perception. It might be his energy guide who is going to help the child during his sleep to process what had happened during the day. As the child feels the guide, he then might label this experience as the presence of his angel, or a Fairy Godmother – that is already a fantasy, because the child arranged his perceptions into a story he can understand. If at the moment of perception of something (neutral opening/imagination), the focus becomes negative – the result will be fear. Now the child is scared that he perceives something dangerous – he then will further expand his imagination into that area of possibilities. That is still imagination, an open perception. The child now is tuning into some less harmonious beings that are *also* in the room. As the child perceives these negative beings, he might label this experience as the presence of a monster in the closet – that would be a fantasy, a story he arranged the perceptions into.

Fantasy is imagination, unrestricted by reality – and I do not just mean material reality here, any reality – and there are many! Opening to possibilities is imagination, allowing them to arrange themselves into a pattern is a teaching tool of Spirit that our Soul applies through the imagination onto our Selves. But an arrangement of these possibilities into a story, something that we ourselves come up with based on our previous Ego or Lower Self experiences – that is fantasy.

Imagination can also be expressed through stories such as *fairytales*. In fact, it is a basic way of training for enhancing one's imagination to listen to a narrative of a fairytale in which the exactness of the chosen words is the fundamental factor necessary to open perceptions from what is known by the material body's senses to the unknown. Fairytales themselves are fantasies, but they are based on imagination and stimulate imagination, which can lead a person to the true deep meaning of a fairytale, the actual pattern that does exist (although it would not look like the images in the fairytale story). Fantasy is not "bad"; it has its own uses. For example, it helps provide meaning to experiences we have had, helps us to understand the newly acquired information by trying it on, so to speak, through putting it into a story. Fantasy is a fundamental skill through which we make sense of the world and it also plays a key role in the learning process. Fantasy is a process of inventing personal realms within the mind.

For example, a *vision* can be both imagination and fantasy: the perception of expansion, feelings of connectedness, colors – these are patterns arranged by imagination, while the "I walked in a field of a tall grass in my vision" is a fantasy, existent to help us explain and anchor the meaning of the vision.

Visualization is one of the ways to experience imagination. In visualization perceived images are seen with the "mind's eye" – i.e. the sixth chakra which is located at the forehead.

Harmonious focus visualization (visual imagination) is highly beneficial for the purposes of personal enlightment. This type of visualization requires the effort of focusing on higher vibratory frequencies. Prior to any visualization, one has to tune into/focus on the expansion of their consciousness, on the purity of beauty, harmony, providence – this can be accomplished through quiet alignment, through prayer (although there are exceptions) or other honest aspiration. Even if one does not know "how" to do it, if sincere intent is present, it begins to flood the energy system with the pure harmony of higher vibrations, which in turn affects the physical brain. The brain then receives energetic imprints from other energy bodies, and provides you with a picture that *translates* that energy (i.e. you are now seeing the pattern that you had allowed to be shown to you). <u>The visual image you are seeing is a code for the explanation of the frequency</u>. For example, you see golden light – this is a translation of purified conceptual Self. Or you see a golden key – this is a translation of a message for a "conceptual solution" to some issue you have needed help with. But when we think in literal material terms, we tend to focus on the "thing" instead of the "what this thing means".

In imagination/visualization everything is a concept – through it we learn to decode the expanded Reality of the Soul.

Imagination does not have to be only visual either. One person might have an easier time "seeing" the light/pictures, while another might feel them more than see, or sense them through their body, or hear the energy of the light/picture. The main goal here is to open these multiple senses, not to "see energy". The seeing might happen for some people, but not for everyone. We all have some extra-sensory abilities, and imagination/visualization is one of the ways to help them open. The extra-sensory perception one might be able to use during visualization is based on one of the physical senses that we have the least amount of fear connected to. And it is not always the same sense we use on a daily basis.

For example, someone might be very visual in their life, but have so much fear attached to "seeing something that is not
78

physical" that they could not use the visual sense in visualization at all! But if this person has almost no fear attached to hearing, they might be able to hear the energy with some success. Or someone might be very physical in their life, but this also limits their perception of the physical senses to the range of the physical world, which would make them unable to sense through their body anything non-physical. But that same person might have less fear attached to the sense of smell, and so they might find themselves smelling different frequencies (harmony might smell like snow, unconditional love like lilies, angelic energy like chocolate chip cookies ☺).

At the beginning of practicing visualization one might want to use "props" to guide them. It can be a soundtrack with a guided meditation, or beautiful music/sounds without the story – either one of these will guide a person on a visual "quest". If you are not sure at all how to do this, start with a guided story-type meditation recording, then progress to listening to only the sounds or music – try to imagine what colors, smells, taste and sensations these sounds have, which might form into the imagery of a story, or remain pure color. Mozart feels very different than Bach, right? Flute sounds resonate differently in the body than trumpets, or nature sounds... Practice perceiving with all five senses. Once this becomes somewhat easy, let go of the guiding tether and allow your own system to guide you. Your being has its own messages for you, your Higher Self, your Soul, your energy guides – all have something to deliver to your consciousness. So let them walk with you on your inner journey of Self-discovery. This is the opening of the inner Creator – we are meant to create realities, and then explore them.

No matter what limited trapped thoughts we have, they could never produce true high frequency visualization, only the fantasy of entrapment. <u>Visualization is always in harmony and is always related to the bigger picture of our lives.</u> You can tune into the faster or slower frequencies, but either way you are looking at the bigger picture – there are no enemies, even the less conscious entities are a part of the whole, and nothing can ever harm you. If during your guided quest you end up taking a turn into some "dark space" with negative imagery that forms into a scary story for you, it is your fear creating the pictures, *fantasizing* about the "what if"… Fantasy can be a good training tool for imagination expansion and visualization, but fantasy is connected to the lower brain – it can only show us (or be made up based on) what we already know. True imagination is about going beyond the known, expanding, harmonizing and finding the Higher Self through the application of the Higher Mind.

The Higher Mind

Being able to believe in non-physical reality means "not being in Ego control", and this goes against our genetic survival programming. We have developed an Ego so we can survive. Without it we feel "naked". But Ego is matter-body based. If we remember that we are more than the body, then we gain access to the Higher Mind of the rest of us! The Ego is a lens, a portal to the Higher Mind, it allows us to be self-aware. But if the Ego associates itself with the lower frequencies, it is stuck in survival programming.

The lower mind that we label Ego is concerned with survival of the body, while the Higher Mind is concerned with the purpose of existence.

Until one begins to ask questions like "why am I here?", "Is there life beyond the physical? Life after death?", "What is

Source/God?" and so on, one cannot begin a journey towards enlightment. These purpose-related questions take us beyond the limitation of the body-self.

How does one start to access the Higher Mind? Visualizations and asking appropriate questions are both good starting points.

The Higher Mind connects to the pure energy. The White Light is the purest energy we can relate to from the inside of density. Originally this entire Universe was all White Light, but in order for it to understand itself, in order for us to become individuals, this White Light had split into many colors, which determine levels within dimensions and dimensions themselves. The colors are the tools for learning about the Self, while the White Light itself is the pure Source energy as we can perceive it. White Light energy is the visual aspect of divine essence of Source, the Light/Word/Code of Divine Intelligence, and it is the most transformational and healing energy in this Universe.

Try to do this every day, pick a time when you will not be disturbed, you might need only fifteen minutes for this visualization. Relax your physical body, close your eyes (you can use a blindfold if you are doing it during the day), and visualize White Light all around you. If you are standing or sitting upright, you can imagine it as a white waterfall. If you are lying down, you might want to imagine yourself in a sphere of white light. Use all the physical senses as much as you can master: see the white light all around you, sense it on your skin and inside your body as you inhale it, hear it surrounding you, taste it, try to smell it. Do so without moving your body. You might only perceive the light with one of the senses at first, but if you do this every day, more senses will begin to perceive the White Light. At that point your brain is in full experience of the White Light, activating dormant areas, which then create a state of calm and peace in your entire physical body. You will notice how your body begins to look forward to these White Light visualizations as moments of relaxation, de-stressing, peace. This will influence your body systems and over time you will see the affects like getting a better handle on stress, better health, more inner calm, and perhaps "unusual to your personality" thoughts and perceptions. That is because the purity of the White Light activates the Higher Mind.

The Higher Mind is all about "purpose" and "meaning," therefore ask yourself these types of questions. If you have difficulty deciding on an action, do not simply analyze the situation, but look at how this action would fit into the bigger picture of your life – what does it mean for you to make that step, or not make it? Anytime we ask larger questions, we active the Higher Mind.

Discernment and Self-Mastery

Self-mastery requires two things: a Self, and discernment. Discernment by going within and tuning into what resonates with our personal truth allows our journey of self-discovery to proceed more smoothly. This discernment comes naturally to each human being once we learn to tune in more to our inner world, and listen to the higher guidance (of our Higher Self and of the beings who are in alignment with that part of us). The more we practice going within, the easier it becomes to discern the guidance of the Higher Mind from the desires and guidance of the Lower Mind. We can always recognize where the guidance came from by the results that it brings, when followed.

We learn to listen to our higher guidance by looking within. This takes practice if you are not used to it. Sitting in silence and listening to your Self – how does your body feel, what thoughts come up, what feelings? Allowing this to keep going for a while will eventually take one past the everyday concerns into the depth of Self.

Sitting in the Great Silence helps us recognize our own personal truth resonance, which allows us to develop discernment.

How do you know what is right for you? Most people never ask this question because they do not know that the answer is *inside*. They tend to either do what everyone around them does without ever questioning it, or they research what is "the best thing out there" according to some group of people or an expert in that field, and follow that direction. But with so many options today it is essential to have discernment from within. When we do what everyone does, we are asleep, there is no self-awareness at that point, and a person is on autopilot of their karma. When we blindly follow what someone else says is the "best thing", we give away our authority. This is detrimental to self-development. There are hundreds of healing modalities available for us today, but only through inner discernment will we know if homeopathy is right for us, or if we need to use traditional allopathic medicine, or whether we need to practice a particular healing technique or not. As we become more and more self-aware and listen to our personal truth resonance, we become able to know which information is good for us. Discrimination within the mass of available information (books, medical research, channelings, internet, different teachers, research) leads to us absorbing only what is right for us.

Why is this important? First of all, all information is neutral. People are in different stages of development and it makes sense that what one person is already ready for, the other one is not. So, it is we who make the information "good" or "bad" based on what we experience in relationship to receiving it, examining it, and perhaps even following it. Even something that is a mis-information can still be of benefit to someone during a particular step on their journey. Secondly, when we take information in and choose to follow it, it is a "correction on the path" of who we are. Just think about it, wouldn't you feel differently if you read an article that said that "all there is to life is materiality and after death there is nothing left of you", vs. reading an article by someone who went through a near-death experience and remembers seeing her family on the other side? One person believes life to be material only; the other one believes there is life after death. There is no right or wrong perception here, but if you try on these beliefs, you will feel one way from the former, and the other way from the later. This is why it is so important to only take in, fully, what benefits you as a being. <u>When you wholly resonate with something, it changes you, and it is your responsibility to be changed in the direction that benefits your essence, not your karma.</u> When we do something out of fear, which means we resonate with our karma, or social beliefs, we take in something that supports these instead of our essence.

When one practices discernment, one feels the path. There is an inner knowing that everything is unfolding perfectly (even if it is hard!) and it frees a person to honor and love the choices of others (cleans up judgment).

There are three stages of progress in the development of such discernment:

1- When we do not resonate with some information, or people, we judge them as wrong, because we believe ourselves to be right, or we doubt ourselves instead;

2- When we do not resonate with information, or people, we choose to not judge and not interact – it is a way of keeping your personal space resonating your own way, while others are resonating their way in their own space (instead of judging a TV show, don't watch it; instead of judging a person, do not talk with them);

3- When we do not resonate with information, or people, and we know that they are following their own path and we follow ours, we can co-exist without being triggered. We recognize and accept the differences and choose to exist in harmony, knowing that we all play unique roles, all learning in accordance with a much larger "perfect" plan.

Gliding in the Prana Current

As I have defined before, prana is pure Energy, the undifferentiated life force. It interpenetrates all existence, all aspects of the Universe "breathe" prana.

Rhythmical connected breaths allow us to experience the force that drives the breath – our divine essence, the Soul-Self. Connecting with it leads us into an experience of love, joy, bliss (magnetically) and peace, silence, purity of the Code resonance (electrically).

Prana/life force is not oxygen, it rides on the oxygen molecule, but it can also ride on other molecules. At this stage of human evolution we require oxygen for our matter-body to function, thus the most digestible prana for us is oxygen-related. Disease cannot exist in a highly oxygenated environment. If we breathe slowly and deeply, we ingest more oxygen to regenerate and harmonize our matter-body, but we also ingest more prana/life force this way. Prana revitalizes the cellular structures of our matter-body and supports de-aging and longevity.

If you think of prana flow as a current, then slow rhythmic breathing without pauses allows you to be carried by that current.

Fine slow breathing (after a long exhale begin a long inhale right away) is more beneficial than sharp breaths or long pauses when we forget to breathe. If we reduce the number of breaths per minute from 15-20 to 3-5, we will triple our lifespan! That is because we ingest more prana with the oxygen.

Attempt slow rhythmic breathing, where you extend your belly in and out (like yoga breath) and if you carry on like this for a while, you will notice that you do not need to pay attention to doing it – the action becomes automatic – that is because you fell in sync with the prana current.

This is a great exercise to engage in when you are off balance (stuck in traffic, or angry, or hurt) because by focusing on the rhythmic slow breaths (let's say, count to seven on inhale and seven on exhale) you will bring in more prana/life force, synchronize with the prana current, and feel yourself harmonizing. You might not feel tranquility right then and there, but you will find your inner balance again so you can deal with the situation in the most beneficial manner. This exercise is also a great preventative measure, if done daily, it releases cumulative stress build up, and with it, any potential disease.

Living inside the prana current of life allows one's "avatar", the matter-body, the experience of harmony. In that state the body's cellular structures are repaired when needed and regenerated, and general health and vitality is present. Prana current also repairs the tears and holes in the energy field, and helps maintain an electromagnetic force field around us – a healthy boundary.

Internal Alchemy

Alchemy is the process of transforming one substance into another: fear into courage, hate into love, greed into generosity, anxiety into peace. This is internal alchemy. One of the first steps of the awakening process is the internal alchemy of turning what is held in our unconsciousness into awareness. This means the transfiguration of the Mundane Lower Self into the Divine Higher Self. Obviously, this is a life-long process. As we change a negative/disharmonic pattern into a life-affirming positive one, we become more conscious of the interconnection patterns, of the reason for the existence of these patterns and of our role in these patterns. And through that we become more masterful in acting within the existent patterns, and in creating new ones. Internal alchemy is activated through intention, but it can also be supported by objects and substances. For example, viewing a mandala can facilitate a particular focus, or drinking structured water (water molecules organized in a particular manner by prayer, or by being in a pyramid structure) can do the same. Any substance in excess is not beneficial, but in a "homeopathic dose" it can be used for transfiguration.

This is the summary of the Mundane Lower Self attributes:

1- needs to have control over circumstances;
2- demands rational explanations (proof);
3- seeks safety/protection at all costs;
4- wants limitation, doesn't risk;
5- references only the past to calculate the future.

This is the summary of the Divine Higher Self attributes:

1- seeks learning/experiences;
2- wants expanded awareness;
3- holds wisdom/higher perspective;
4- allows for perceptional freedom/openness;
5- exists in each current moment fully.

In order to expand more of our consciousness into the Higher Self range, and transmute the limiting beliefs of the Lower Self, use this exercise. For it you will need structured water (*more about it in the "Structured Water" chapter, page 152*).

1- Sit down comfortably and relax. Breathe deeply to bring in the White Light into your energy system while a glass of water is in your hands/in your energy field (no more than three feet from your body).

2- While holding a glass of water in your hand, but BEFORE you take water into your mouth, tune into the emerald green energy in your heart chakra.

3- Then chose one of your negative attributes (anger, arrogance, worthlessness, depression, rigidity, blaming, overwhelm, etc.) to transmute – you will be releasing it, letting it go.

4- *A:* if you prefer a structural/more mental/electric method: use your intent/will/focus to allow the water to transmute that attribute as you swallow. Then experience this transmutation as the water works through your system.

B: if you prefer a fluid/more emotional/magnetic method: become loose/wave-like and, as you swallow the water, feel it softening and transmuting this attribute in your system.

Is-ness and Illusions

This is a very complex subject and requires a book of its own, but I will summarize the main points here. Understanding these concepts is essential to personal awakening.

There is one True Reality that is ***Spirit/Source/ Is-ness*** – All That Is. ***Is-ness is Holographic*** in nature. The term *hologram* is comprised of the Greek words *holos* (whole) and *gramma* (message). Hologram is a condition upon which the information for creating a whole system is stored in each of its parts. Hologram is a pattern that is whole and complete all to itself, which is part of a pattern, that is whole and complete to itself, and so on. Every, even the smallest, change made within a hologram, is mirrored throughout the entire hologram. Our planet, the genetic code in our bodies, our Universe – all are holographic in nature.

Conceptually Is-ness/Spirit is a Divine Trinity: the "Root Cosmic Substance" aspect, the "Creator" aspect, and the "Light/Word/Code" aspect.

"Root Cosmic Substance" is the Spirit's material for Creation. This is why people say "all is Love" – this component is what we

91

label pure Divine Love. It is the potentiality of the harmonious creation of everything. Energy/prana/Ether, as the support life force, is this substance, it is the "supply of the Source".

"*Creator*" is the Spirit's original spark for Creation. Energy/prana/Ether, as enlivening life force, is this component, it is the "aliveness of the Source," the initial "Spark of God".

"*Light/Word/Code,*" or Logos, is the Symbiosis of Creation, it is the super- system of symbiotic arrangement of the Universal Laws, a Holographic Source-Code that allows meanings to be generated, circulated, and interpreted. It is the Divine Intelligence, the "Unity Consciousness."

Root Cosmic Substance & Creator & Light/Word/Code →

Souls ("Gods in training")

Souls are individualized expressions of holographic Is-ness – composites of Root Cosmic Substance and the Creator energies, playing in the Light/Word/Code of Unity Consciousness. Each Soul creates its own reality through its own perception, in order to explore the Source-Code and become God again. Through this exploratory process Souls gain self-awareness, enriching Source/Spirit/Is-ness with consciousness (an awareness of its own existence).

In order to awaken into godhood we generate realities and explore them. One reality is not any more or less real than others. They all are "experiments" and "simulations" for the benefit of our awakening.

In StarTrek there is a wonderful concept called the *holodeck*, which beautifully explains this process. A holodeck is an electromagnetic grid imbedded in a room, able to project photonic simulation of material reality. Photon is a subatomic particle that carries the electromagnetic force, with zero mass but has measurable momentum, exhibits deflection by a gravitational field, and can exert a force. It has no electric charge, has an indefinitely long lifetime, and is its own antiparticle. With reference to the holodeck, these photons are arranged by a "holo-novel", which is a story written for the holodeck – it is a program that runs on the grid of the holodeck, filled with environments and characters, and people can go in and experience this holo-novel as if they walk into a movie, but they can interact with the characters, and because it is a computer program, the characters adapt to the human participants – sort of like a much more sophisticated computer game than is available today.

Looking at this from the StarTrek's holodeck analogy, the Root Substance would be the electro-magnetic energy that runs through the holodeck, the Creator would be the photonic energy, the Light/Word/Code would be the structure of the holodeck itself (the gird), and the author of a holo-novel would be the Soul, while the participants in that holo-novel (people who actually walk in and experience the story) would be us, the "avatars" of our Souls experiencing the "simulation" of reality.

There is only one reality – Is-ness. When we have merged our awareness with All That Is, we are multidimensional, we are everything. This is a concept, and when one takes on this concept, tries it on wholly, there is recognition that everything else is an illusion. This does not mean that "nothing is real", in fact, everything is real! But once you know that what you really are is everything, you understand that all the self-created programs around you are an illusion. They are the Light/Word/Code, but modified, amplified or subdued, twisted in every which way. You also understand that these illusions serve a purpose – they help us figure ourselves out. Every illusion is a form of perceptional separation from the whole. Just like we, as Souls, have created these separations, we now have to figure out ways of lifting the veils and returning to the whole. Inside our illusions we have built a concept of God being outside of ourselves. It is a necessary component of awakening. But as we begin to remember that all is linked, that God is in everything, we create holes in the illusion and the Light shines through.

All the systems within this Universe/God – the dimensional divisions, the voids, the spiritual hierarchies, the angels, the "helpful" or not ETs, the energy guides and even our own Higher Selves – all are illusions, but necessary ones. Without them we will not be able to fully remember who we are. Think of it like a computer game: environment and characters are created, so that the player can go through certain experiences and "win", move up to the next level of skill. Children learn mathematics not because it is going to be a required skill in life when they grow up (most of us just use calculators!), but because it allows the brain to grow neuron pathways in particular ways which will make this child smarter, more capable of dealing with complex problems, when he/she grows up. We teach our children different skills, and the ones which are not really necessary for life when they grow up are necessary for their development into smart, capable individuals. Same with the exploration of this Universe/God: Souls generate "realities" in order for us to grow and develop, but all these "realities" are illusions in comparison to the one True Reality of Is-ness.

Self Eternal

Our pure essence, the Soul-Self, is formless – it is pure consciousness. This formless component of Spirit lives in a multitude of forms; it desires, creates and explores through these forms in different dimensions. A dimension is an energy consciousness range where learning is set to particular rules; each dimension has twelve levels – in that a dimension is similar to an octave and the levels to separate notes (*more detailed explanation of levels and dimensions is in my book "Mission Alpha."*)

We all essentially are one being. This unified state maintains a "design", the Universal Divine Mind of the Light/Word/Code. This component is a shared unified consciousness, but it is individually accessed through one's Divine Mind. You can say it is all one intelligence, but it can be experienced as a field of information of any and all subjects, and also as an individual path inside that large design. The Universe is a *hologram, and our Soul-Selves are its fractal aspects.*

Each life-form is a fractal aspect of a hologram of symbiotic evolution.

Fractal is a detailed pattern, a self-similar (macro and micro) aspect/unit of a hologram which contains the entire pattern of the hologram within itself.

We are unlimited beings choosing to live inside a limited environment (dimension, star system, body) in order to learn about ourselves. We are all "Gods in training" and we are also all "God" (as in "calibrated with Spirit of this Universe"). We are "powered" by Spirit/God. It is so no matter if we pay attention to it or not,

95

believe it or not – It Is. This "state of Is-ness" remains constant and is never separate from us (because we are it!) but our beliefs of separation generate <u>perceptory separation</u>, which then becomes our experience. Our limited beliefs are here for a reason – they are the parameters for our experiences (dimensional parameters are a form of limitation, duality is a limitation, any form, even a star or a galaxy, is a limitation). Transmuting these limited beliefs allows us expansion of perceptory parameters, eventually leading to full awakening – being All That Is (experiencing Is-ness).

This expanded state of being can be experienced by focusing on a pure point of momentary presence – the Now. Materially we have to move along a linear timeline but in states of stationary meditation this state of pure being-ness can be experienced. This experience of focusing on Is-ness is not emotional – it goes beyond joy and bliss. The Is-ness can be experienced as pure Unconditional Love, and/or as Perfect Design (depending on how each entity is inclined perceptionally).

The higher places of existence, or our own Soul-Self, does not reach out to us – it is the other way around, we must reach out towards it. When we do, we become more and more aware of the multidimensional aspects of ourselves. But it is our choice to take this journey – no one else can make you do it or do it for you. As we realize that we are on a journey of awakening, our free will determines through which lenses will we look at this journey – what perception are we choosing: resistance, victim, fear and anguish (all based on a concept of external authority controlling the journey – child/parent view) or excitement, responsibility, joy and mastery (all based on the authority within – the "grown up" view). Because each of us awakens through resonating with our personal unique Divine Soul-Self (soul signature), it is essential that we find a way to that particular resonance. How? Our resonance consists of broadcasts via beliefs, thoughts, emotions, and actions. And so every choice we make, from the dietary and sleep levels, to practical research, to the internal investigation level – all of these steps alter our broadcasts.

As we awaken, unresolved emotions are processed, limited thoughts are linked to limited beliefs and transmuted, and the survival strategies of the Lower Self are released. At this stage the Ego (our operating personality which normally tends to listen to the Lower Self) allies with the Higher Self. In a sense we "become the Higher Self", we act from that place. At this stage of awareness we are experiencing the interconnectedness of all life, and the desire to be of service to ourselves and others. Unconditional love becomes a natural feeling and all lower emotions are easily transmuted. The knowledge of how life works (appropriate to the dimension we are in) acts like a constant blueprint for our creations – this is the alignment with our Divine Mind in that dimension. This stage is a mastery of Self in form, and it repeats through many experiments we go through, in many dimensions of our existence (mastery of the third-dimensional Self, then mastery of the fourth-dimensional Self, and so on). A state of enlightment marks an arrival to a self-mastery point, which propels up into the next experiment. Awareness creates awareness. Conscious vigilance for opportunities of growth allows us to recognize them with more ease, each time becoming less and less limited.

With completion of each mastery level we gain abilities. For example, completion of our current third-dimensional experiment will gift us with abilities like bi-locating, teleportation, clairvoyance and clairaudience, telepathy and distant viewing. These might seem extreme for the current material view point, but enlightment "beyond this dimension" into the fourth dimension will allow us to experience these abilities here in the third dimension, and some on the lower levels of fourth. But if we want to acquire more abilities, they will be ours after achieving mastery of the fourth dimension. As we proceed through our multidimensional awakening, we are still bound by the Law of Karma, and in some instances we reincarnate (although not always into material forms as what we now label "matter"). The more advanced we are in our journey, the more "immortal" we feel – even though reincarnation and karma might still affect us, there is a conscious continuity. The energy is consistent, it cannot be destroyed, it only changes form. We are the consciousness that rides on the waves of this Universal Harmony, frolicking and playfully enjoying the spiral of experience.

For example, in this reality we do not remember our past and future lives. In a few very rare instances some people do, which always is paired with a very particular Soul Contract. Usually a person needs to apply some amount of conscious work in order to remember, but it still will not be a "full memory" of the reincarnational journey. Yet the closer to the harmony of Source we are, the more memory we retain/awaken about our journey. Therefore a being in the fifth dimension might still have a need to change forms because of karmic lessons, but will have a much more tangible experience of the Soul-Self that is a constant throughout these lifetimes.

As we become synchronized with the flow of Universal Creation, our own part in it comes full circle:

Creator → *Creative Expression* →

Co-Creator → *Creation.*

Creator and its creation are the same – the Is-ness flavored with uniqueness of desires.

What happens when we arrive at "the end" of this journey? Since we are in a linear mind perception right now and think in finalities, we can entertain the idea of "the end" – let's think of it as "return to Source". What happens when we have mastered our Selves in every dimension that we chose to play in? We then transcend into yet another level of awareness, where there is no form, where we fully experience ourselves as pure consciousness. In many higher dimensions there is "no form" from our material view point. But being a consciousness of a galaxy is still a "type of form", is it not? So what we are talking about here is beyond ANY form in ANY dimension. That is the state of Is-ness, of "I Am" – the Divine Soul-Self.

Merging with the Is-ness, becoming the Divine Self, frees us from any form, from any karma (it has all been dealt with), from reincarnation of any kind – we become eternal (immortal in a true sense). Here we can choose to experience this Universe in any way we like, materializing and dematerializing in the lower dimensions, manifesting any forms in the higher, becoming any expression of any being (sort of "riding the wave" of their experience) – we become limitless (within this Universe). At that point some leave this Universe to create their own universes, although the majority of these Source beings remain "creator-gods" of this Universe.

Personal Reality

Each person perceives reality differently because each of us is unique (genetically, psychologically, emotionally, karmically).

Genetic/Psychological/Emotional/Karmic

make up + Current Attitude/Belief =

Emotional Reaction/Thought/Action →

Creation of <u>*Personal Reality*</u> *(as life mirrors*

what we projected out back to us).

Our personal reality is created through the *way* we see life. It is based on previous experiences, beliefs we hold, cellular memory, subconscious influences from other lives and much more. And all of this is also affected by our current attitude, the lens through which we choose to view life. This lens triggers emotional responses, thoughts and actions. And since it is our reality, we then attract to us what resonates with our internal perceptions. This is how we create our personal reality.

The Higher Mind/Reason is derived from Spirit. We can use the Higher Mind as a path to lead us into Spirit. Imagine you are lost in the desert. How do you know where to go? You can randomly start walking, perhaps you can examine all information available to you and then decide where to go, or you can follow one of many paths left in the sand by others. This is where you really need to use your discernment in order to pick the direction appropriate for you. Unfortunately most people just wander in circles. Few people make their own unique path. The rest follow the paths that already exist. There is no right or wrong choice here – choosing to leave the desert is already a form of awakening. Using inner guidance to tune in and know what is the <u>correct path for you</u> is the most important component.

We must not set our standard of "normal" according to another's perception. The ability to claim what we perceive as real and investigate it, determining if it is beneficial to us or not (sometimes we have to become it in order to know) is the only way to find our own path, our own destiny.

No one else's path will be your own. You can choose to trace someone else's path as a means of "lifting the veil", to support your own expansion of consciousness, but at some point you will have to stand in your own truth.

When we follow someone else's path to that point, but instead of claiming our own perception insist on "this path itself is the only true path", we get lost instead of lifting the veil of illusion. Claiming personal truth might be one of the hardest things to ever have to do. Why? When we are exploring the lower realms of illusion, we are supported by the multitudes of other people

102

traveling on the same path. Even if the path itself is not conventional, there might be more than enough people on it for you to feel safe – as a part of a spiritual community, part of a church group, or an ashram, or a group of skeptics.

But once you get to the veil itself, to the point of breakthrough, unless you let go of the group's beliefs and walk alone – you won't lift the veil. There are some things that we can only do alone – this is one of them.

No one can pierce through the Illusion within a group – this step has to be individual. We must go it alone...

It is all the more difficult to take this step if your truth is perceived by others as unconventional and even "crazy". This is the point of "trial", the "test" that all spiritual traditions talk about – can you stand in your own perceptional truth, your own personal reality, even if you are alone? If you can, you make your perceptional truth your reality. If it is an expanded truth, one way or the other connected to the Higher Self, than this new reality you enter would be harmonious and will benefit your spiritual development. The beliefs and realities of other people are there for us to reflect upon – they are the triggers for asking the proper questions, which are meant to clarify our own path.

If society blindly conforms to the norms of the ancestors without adjustments, it stagnates. If we follow the accepted norm, we become limited by the perceptory range of others.

Change only comes from daring to be different!

When we claim what we perceive as real, even if it goes against the norm, we create a point of reference of what is possible, which serves us and others in awakening. We have an innate Code for progress, for discovery – this is how we awaken. But everyone is different and one person might be having a "need to explore and know" lifetime, while another might be having a "rest" lifetime. We all take these rest lifetimes, when we just coast along, not making any waves.

But everyone occasionally has a lifetime when they are due to make a very big wave (some more often than others). Not everyone is curious about the working of the cells, or the atomic composition of matter, or life on other planets... But some are and their persistent belief in their personal truth is what allows us all to become a little bit more awake. If people hadn't gone traveling, they would not have found other cultures, different from their own. If someone hadn't choosen to go into the open seas, we would never have found other continents. If someone hadn't built a telescope, looked into it, and then claimed that what he saw was real, we would never have known that the Earth is round and that it rotates around the Sun. Human history (and any other material planetary history) is always based on the ones who "rock the boat" of conventional norm.

Unfortunately the saying "ignorance breeds fear" is very true... If someone is in thier Lower Self, they will feel fear in relation to what they cannot understand. If one is in their Higher Self, they will feel curiosity instead! But one "cannot get there from here" – it is not possible to just switch from fear to curiosity without the intermediate step – the Self. This is why knowledge and self-awareness of personal reality is so important, without it we are trapped in fear-based surviving. In the higher truth, every perception is valid. We tend to fear what we do not understand because our Lower Self, trapped in survival, lives in duality and believes that "if they are right, I must be wrong" and thus it judges the other's perceptional truth as "wrong" and dangerous. Yet every "simulated reality" is here to inspire us to awaken. Someone might have to hate, to kill, to betray in order to become a harmonious Self, while someone else might have already passed that stage and now perceives more of the bigger picture, hence the knowledge that by harming another we only harm ourselves. But no one can just tell someone that – they have to go through the required steps of direct experience in order to comprehend that concept.

Every "personal reality" is here to teach the one who is experiencing it. If we come in contact with that someone and their world interferes with ours, it is our lesson now. When we have learned and do not require this lesson anymore, we will either not be triggered by that person, or we will navigate away from them in such a way that they can still have their perception and we can have ours.

The way we perceive life dictates the nature of our personal reality. Our perceptions are influenced by previous experiences, but they can be changed by the means of self-awareness of our inner beliefs about life. We all have an inherent ability to shape reality through our thoughts (concepts). Fully embodied knowledge of that is the first step in self-mastery and the creation of life that we desire.

Earth as a Living Library

Our planet is alive and she is a repository of knowledge of the Universe. We come into the Earth Experiment to experience this library, to study its material and to learn. Some will study only one subject for many lifetimes, others skip around, most resist studying all together, few will have curiosity about who built the library, and even fewer will know the answer and want to improve on the material stored in the library.

All paths are ok – it is the way life is. We are all "special," there is no competition in specialness! It is as important to study one subject as it is to study many, or to skip about. It is ok to resist too. But eventually we all must get to the point of awakening – know that we are in a library, study what is available and recognize who built it. Some will awaken studying only one subject (maybe science, or medicine, or spiritual tradition), others will study more than one. Everyone will have to learn self-discipline and eventually stop resisting this learning, but very few will be the ones to add to/improve the library. And it is all ok.

Combining an open mind, trust in our perception, with research and personal experience allows us to choose our path inside this Earth's library wisely.

Knowing the Spirit

Our personal reality is constructed from the top down. It begins with an overall belief about something, which generates thoughts on that subject, out of which come the emotions. This sequence influences our perception of reality. We must be responsible for that internal process in order to awaken.

Belief → Thought → Emotion → Reality

Our thoughts are based on our conceptual understanding of reality. Concepts are energetic programs – we call these "beliefs". And what we believe – we create. Our thoughts come out of our beliefs.

We have the power to control our thinking, and in that to change our reality.

When we have an emotion we do not like, it is not because of what has triggered that emotion into existence outside of us, it is because of the belief and the thought patterns that we hold on the inside. The external trigger is just that – a trigger, it is not a cause.

Emotions are designed as the "default triggers" for the choosing of the path. What this means is that emotions are secondary to Knowing the Code, but because humanity does not know God/Source Code right now, it must feel.

We have emotions only because we do not know the Design Code of the Source.

One of the definitions of "code" in a dictionary is "a system of symbols and rules used to represent instruction, a base program". Everything is essentially a code – this entire Universe exists by Light/Word/Code. For example, Joy is a program that comes from the Creator, while Bliss is a component of the Root Substance. Both are primary codes of Creation. But when we do not know how to read that code, we have other means of experiencing it – feelings. This is why we consider joy and bliss to be feelings – they are base programs and one of the ways to experience them (the one most readily available on Earth) is feeling.

Most people have an emotional reaction to stimuli instantaneously – they feel powerless in front of that reaction, it runs them. This emotional reaction is an activation of an internal program that is not harmonious – it is asking for our help in its balancing. There is nothing wrong in having an emotional reaction, but there is a problem if one keeps having the same reaction over and over. This means that a trigger brought up an issue that this person is not choosing to deal with – the issue will just keep coming up then until it receives attention!

When most people have an emotional reaction, they do not stop to investigate, instead they act. But their action is based on the emotional reaction, in other words, it does not lead to awakening, only to a recycling of the same karmic pattern over and over. Once we have an emotion, we can immediately investigate which thought pattern it was based on, and then change the pattern if it is not beneficial – this will lead to a different action. This investigation and a different action are steps on the path of life that we agreed to take – this is how we awaken.

Each person's path is unique and all paths have the right to exist. But this is only true applied to "walking the path". When someone does not like their path, they can't just get off because they do not like the scenery! Before coming here we had agreed to walk on our path – we "signed a contract", the Soul Contract. By doing so we became a piece of the planetary puzzle, a component that is now incorporated into the current Earth experiment. If we do not walk our path, we interfere with the planetary evolution as a whole. Looking for one's path counts, it is better than not doing anything.

Walking the path is the only way to awaken. But quite often people just give in to their fears and stop – in a sense they sit down on the road and refuse to move. That is not ok – it is detrimental to us and the planet. We have a purpose and that purpose is linked to us walking the path. When we refuse to do it (and there is always fear behind the stubbornness), we immediately drown in our karma and genetic memory. Taking a break on the path can be necessary, especially if what you are going through feels very hard to you. But a "rest stop" is not the same thing as stopping and refusing to get up when it is time.

How do you know the difference between the "rest stop" and the refusal to move? Simple: "rest stop" is NOT an avoidance of the path; it is a way to take care of oneself (and the part of the Self that we take care of is NOT the Lower Self!) It can be very beneficial to allow yourself a break in processing of some emotional pain, or in dealing with a difficult problem. But these breaks are not open-ended; they have parameters for when we will resume the work. When we attempt to avoid our life because it is too hard, because we do not like it, because we do not believe we can live it – as soon as we stop, all our fears and issues surround us.

Activation of the Elemental Forces

Initially, through the intense curiosity of the Soul, a descent into density is activated. Curiosity is the quality that makes space for the exploration. The Cosmic Root Substance opens to meet the Creator, generating "Divine Blueprint" (Light/Word/Code), in which the Soul constructs forms to explore through. A Soul then generates a Light Body – a Blueprint/Code of itself, a vehicle for multi-dimensional exploration. Thus, through the journey of exploration of different densities, the divine Soul imprint (its energy signature, its uniqueness) is activated.

As the Soul enters the conceptual reality of Earth, the Elemental forces of creation are activated in sequence inside the human body matrix. This ensures the proper ability to awaken when the time is right. Every person is comprised of a precise combination of the elements needed for their evolution in matter (*you can read about this in detail in "Mission Alpha", chapter "Elements"*), but we all have all five elements as the anchor points for being in matter in the first place. On Earth we utilize these five elements as we grow:

1- In the womb – Water Element is linked into the body-being.

2- During birth – Air Element is linked. The first independent breath of the new being activates an individual unique electro-magnetic circuitry in the body of the infant. Simultaneously, the geometric Soul design (one's own complex Soul Symbol) is encoded on the Earth's Memory Grid, and the astrological imprint is overlaid into the Light Body. This is the "announcement" that a new life form has incarnated.

3- Activated body-senses – Earth Element is linked. Waves of time passing, in combination with information-infused Light, gives direction to the bio-signaling systems of the human hologram/body/being, as the Earth circles the Sun. This circular cycling: days, nights, months, seasons, decades...on and on, is necessary for growth experience. This cycling/spiraling changes us, like a diamond emerging from coal. This movement, and repetitive process, reinforces our Divine human destiny as the universal perpetuator of Life. We continue becoming an integral part of the Universal material plane, intrinsically belonging to it, because of these on-going cycles/spirals of time.

4- Desire – Fire Element is linked. Throughout each lifetime, if we are brave, we relate to the Universe with a desire for intimate contact with Life (comprehension and relationship), thus passionately engaging life. The Fire Element is a strong "training partner" for the physical body to become a fully activated matter-vehicle for the spiritual identity to inhabit. As we become more awake and whole, the entire spectrum of the chakras is able to translate Light into ecstatic experience, and dense matter is Light-infused. The Fire Element relates to identity and passion, but can cause the physical body to feel as if occasionally it is being shocked with high voltage electricity. Yet the heat is necessary for the alchemy and our awakening.

5- Spiritual Awakening – Ether (pure Spirit) Element is linked. At the current stage of our development, we humans have not established a full conscious relationship with this Element yet, although this pure energy is becoming more and more active in the planetary matrix itself, which contributes to its conscious experience by more people. This Ether Element is transparent in its pure form, and it becomes colored depending on the flavor of whose consciousness generated it. Practicing tuning into Ether Element in the planet is necessary for activating more of it on the inside of our own systems. One of the easiest ways to tune into this element is by focusing on the stars – the "stellar ether".

These are the steps of an Elemental alchemy. It means that each of us will internally use our own unique design of the Elements, to achieve a different balance point from where we originally began the incarnation.

When we put the Elements together in specific, new and beneficial ways, we heal. Think of the alchemy of baking. Take flour, sugar, salt, eggs, butter, cream, leavening and spices. Mix in the right sequence, apply heat, and you have a wonderful substance to eat. The mixture of the parts creates a magnificent Whole.

Knowing the role of the Elements in our experience allows us another tool for fine-tuning our system. Here is a list of basic Elemental qualities that we experience as humans:

Fire:

- balanced: passion, identity, intensity, direct action;
- over-abundant: anger, hatred, jealousy, drama;
- deficient: disappointment, deflation, no desire.

Air:

- balanced: inspiration, expansion, intellect, mental;
- over-abundant: confusion, ungrounded;
- deficient: boredom, no interest.

Water:

- balanced: peaceful, merging, sensitivity, feeling;
- over-abundant: sluggishness, depression;
- deficient: dissatisfaction, no connection.

Earth:

- balanced: stability, security, presence, being;
- over-abundant: rigidity, stoicism;
- deficient: uncertainty, no safety.

Increasing Personal Light Quantity

Spiritual development is represented in both vibrational frequency and atomic structure. Space between electrons, protons and neutrons changes as the Light expands within the atom. This Light *reflects* a person's awareness of their Divine Soul-Self. As the self-awareness grows, the Light expands to fill the space in each atom, changing the frequency (rate of oscillation) of each atom in the body.

As we increase our awareness, and with it the personal Light quantity within our cellular structure, we become multi-dimensional (able to perceive other dimensions).

Transition into a higher dimensional state is a process. We are not matter one day and Light energy the next. There are exceptional cases when the transition is instantaneous, but one must be ready on all the levels simultaneously, which in itself is rare. If one intends for it, but is not ready, one's "instantaneous transition" might be felt as an electrocution. Our energy fields have to be infused and aligned with Light/Word/Code gradually, as not to experience electrical burn out. The process of building and activating the Light Body is mandatory because it is linked to planetary evolution. Our planet upgrades her Light Body periodically.

The Light Body is not the same as the energy field. Our personal learning is contained in the energy field, while our bigger plans for who we are are contained in the Light Body. We all have one, it is a Soul component. While being on this planet, we "upgrade" our Light body as the planet upgrades hers. As time goes on, the crystalline structures of Earth realign to a higher vibrational tone. Every time the same has to be done by all beings living on the planet at that time. Anyone not wishing to be part of this process at that time, tends to choose death by disease, accident, or a natural disaster. They then join the next life-wave (*more about life-waves in the "Evolutionary Acceleration" chapter, page 183*) and experience the transition when they are ready (on Earth or elsewhere). Earth's environment allows for this, and it is not a "failure" to choose to wait till the next life-wave, there is no judgment involved.

We are transmuting our denser confused energies into Light, and in doing so, becoming more Light ourselves. Some are consciously working on absorbing Light and transmuting disharmony, therefore their Light Body transformation is quicker. Others are unaware, but they are still absorbing Light and experiencing some transmutation, echoing the planet.

The Universe Responds to Our Expectations

We are responsible for our emotional reaction to any event.

All emotional reactions are always based on our conscious/subconscious expectations.

An example of a conscious expectation is wanting a burst of excitement and happiness from a child after you have given her a toy, but she opens the gift, looks at it and moves on, your toy is quickly forgotten. You will experience disappointment in the child, or in yourself for not being able to please that child, to find the right gift. An example of subconscious expectation is failing a class in college and feeling confused, lost, frustrated, thinking that you had done everything to succeed; while in truth internally you had an emotional expectation that you would fail because you are "just not that smart" and so it came true.

Anything that we experience can be polarized into either gratitude or disappointment. It is our Attitude that does the polarization.

When you look at a glass of water filled half way, do you feel it is "half full" or "half empty"? We have an emotional inclination to feel one way or the other, while both statements materially are equally valid.

All events in life are originally emotionally neutral - it is we who attach emotional reactions to them.

For example, you arrived at your vacation hotel of choice, but your luggage has been lost during travel and you will have to wait 48 hours for it to catch up with you. It is a neutral event. One person might have a reaction of anger and spend these 48 hours arguing with the airline and hotel staff. Another person might decide to do some basic shopping and enjoy what the destination has to offer, knowing that their luggage is taken care of.

Negative emotional reactions are <u>contagious,</u> just like the irresponsibility itself. Someone blaming the airline and hotel might attract others who also want to blame something for their anger or unhappiness, because blame is easier than responsibility. It takes no effort to blame. But blame can only be generated by an immature part of us – it is the part that is looking for a parent, someone outside of us, to take care of us, and when we do not feel "taken care of" we look for that "parent" to blame.

It is very important to understand, deeply, that there are no "bad events" no matter how difficult they are for us. Instead there are positive or negative <u>reactions</u> to the events!

The harder the event, the more effort it takes to stay positive. One can go through a very difficult illness, or life circumstance, and feel stronger for it, more sure of themselves than ever.

The opportunity to reprogram ourselves is there in every moment. All we have to do is remember that it is our perception of the event that determines our choice to react positively or negatively. We must look for the thoughts and beliefs that have generated our perception, and start changing them. If this seems too hard right now, then simply go into gratitude – it is a fail-safe for positive emotional reaction. Choosing positive perception benefits us, and others, including the planet.

But having a positive perception does not mean avoiding looking at the issues. Most people have a misconception that "being positive" means not having any negativity. That is avoidance and escape, not true harmony. <u>Being positive means that we choose to face directly our fears and the negative beliefs that created them, and that we dare to challenge these negative inner patterns, eventually bringing them to the harmony of the Higher Self.</u> This is actually how we heal the Lower Self, which is a defensive part of us that is meant to protect us from the world. When we know how interconnected we really are, there is no more need for protection.

Our material bodies hold the memory of experiences that the bodies physically have gone through, but also the ones imprinted from the other lifetimes. When we incarnate, the energy field carries in it all our previous experiences. Even though these have not happened to your current body, they can feel very real to it. For example, someone afraid of flying in an airplane might have fallen off a cliff and experienced a long fall while knowing that death was inevitable, and someone afraid of bridges might have hung himself from a bridge in another life. These intense physiological and emotional responses surface when we are exposed to particular sets of triggers. This design is on purpose – it allows us to reprogram ourselves. For example, someone with the fear of flying must study how airplanes work and why they stay in the air, the sounds during flight, why turbulence occurs, etc. – the use of mental knowledge then calms the emotional body, which in turn calms the physical. And someone who is afraid of bridges can choose to take slow walks over them, notice the beauty of the construction parallel to feeling the fear – this re-sets the emotional and cellular programs, this time without the fear.

The dualistic nature of our existence here on Earth implies experiences of both happiness and unhappiness, health and dis-ease, love and fear. Throughout the lifetimes we choose to play on one side of the spectrum, then the other, sometimes both.

When we are ready to become spiritual adults, we finally choose the middle path – the path of harmony.

By the means of taking full responsibility for every experience we have, and understanding how our perceptions (beliefs, thoughts, emotions) create our reality, we generate the attitude of Self-empowerment, and through it really create our reality.

Perception is a learned skill. As I have mentioned before, that skill is heavily influenced by our genetics, upbringing, and current and past life experiences. All of these are imprinted upon our body's cellular memory. These cellular imprints attract to us the same circumstances over and over, and can be the cause of dis-ease in the body or mind, until we deal with them. Through unconscious

120

habitual repetition we "carve a groove" in our neuro-circuitry, inculcating automated conditioned biochemical responses to be triggered by particular circumstances and people.

All events trigger an emotional response, either positive or negative, according to our perception of that event. The point of self-mastery, the "middle path", lays in being able to *notice* the emotional reaction we are having, *trace it back through the thoughts to the belief (concept) that created it*, and *change* that belief.

You might ask "how do I change the belief/concept once I recognize it?" This takes some inner knowing of your own system, and definitely some effort.

We change our beliefs by resolving the past disharmonious assumptions – the unlearned lessons which created the disharmonious beliefs.

We do this by dealing directly with the past trauma and harmonizing the concept itself – learning what was unlearned, finishing what was not finished.

Dealing directly with the past trauma requires knowledge of Self. Knowledge of Self is gained through internal investigation. The more we know about our inner world, the easier it becomes to trace the origins of any belief. These origins almost always thread from other lives, but there are also many circumstances of the current life that have activated these past karmic issues in our cellular memory. The key here, again, is perception. These unresolved karmic issues were originally created by our misunderstandings of a lesson due to a limited perception at that time. But now we are different beings than we were back then, thus our perceptional range is also different. This means that examining circumstances that lead to a particular belief in the past with this new expanded perspective will lead to a different conclusion, which in turn affects the thoughts and emotions, and the cellular body in a different way.

Most of the time we can trace the emotional reaction to an issue that we can then further delineate back to a particular episode in life that cemented that conclusion into our body. For example, someone who is experiencing intense feelings of unworthiness and insignificance in a current moment due to a particular trigger might be able to trace it back to the time of his parents' divorce and the pain experienced during it. The incorrect conclusion was "If I was good enough, then mommy/daddy would not have left us!" The child took this experience as his fault. If this was not noticed by the adults around him, he grew stronger in his conviction until it became a full belief. From that point on this child would keep attracting to himself triggers for his insignificance because his Soul would want him to learn, to clean up this misconception. By simply looking back at the event itself (in this case, a traumatic divorce) through the eyes of the adult, and consciously linking these two experiences (feeling not-good-enough and parents' divorce), this person can release the pain or guilt, that generated the belief in the first place. Information can be very useful in these situations – knowing about the real reasons for the divorce of his parents, which might have been hidden from the child, can help a lot.

Sometimes we are not able to trace the current issue to anything literal in our past. For example, someone who is afraid to be alone in life, and yet is happily married, and in her memory she has always been surrounded by a large family that loved her, or a nice circle of friends. Yet the fear persists. This person can trace the feeling of fear throughout her life, but with no material circumstance to attach it to. This means it is a karmic issue from another lifetime (they all are, but some have very obvious triggers in this life, others do not). To help release this trauma, this person must tune into the feeling itself and let it be the guide to the constructed "story"/belief. What is the emotion behind the fear? What are the facets of this fear: loneliness, danger, insecurity? By examining these facets a path to the belief is created, and this belief might then be challenged with the current perceptional view. What does it mean to be lonely? Why is it scary? If everyone disappears, who will she be as an individual? Facing these questions will also lead to the release of the karmic overlay and changes in the root belief. The use of meditation (sitting in the Great Silence of Self), consulting professionals in the fields of energy work, healing, breath-work, hypnosis, past life regression, and other modalities can be helpful.

Everything existing in our lives – circumstances and people who trigger us into positive or negative emotional responses – all have been attracted to us by the type of energies (belief/thought/emotion) that we have emitted over lifetimes. Our entire being is a broadcast mechanism. Our physical, emotional, mental and spiritual bodies all put out frequencies – these transmissions are then reflected back to us. These frequencies become trapped in biofeedback loops until we resolve the imbalanced emission issue.

Mind Mastery

Fully embodying the belief that we create our reality frees our consciousness range from self-imposed limitations. This is the first step of the path of Self-Mastery – the mastery of the Mind. We become aware that we are responsible not only for our actions, but also for every thought we have. We then recognize that we must become disciplined in tracking these thoughts to their conceptual origins, and facing head on our fears and misconceptions. At first this process is much harder than the victim way of life, when we simply blame others, the world, or life for our problems. It is difficult and takes incredible vigilance to be able to pay attention to feelings and thoughts – all of them! People who are more mentally inclined might find it easier to track the thoughts, while those more emotionally inclined would find tracking their feelings easier. But in the end the result is the same – it leads us to the origin of the belief (we can feel it, or know it, or remember the actual circumstance) so we can change it.

How do you know you have "mind mastery"? When you feel in the flow in all areas of your life, you know you have graduated this step. Through self-discipline and discernment the quality of one's life improves significantly. You are able to create your life consciously. This does not mean of course that everything will be perfect from now on – remember, this is the "middle path" of internal harmony and balance, of inner peace, but not the "light" per se. Therefore yes, even at this level of mastery one still experiences pain, and other uncomfortable emotions, occasional confusion and unsettling thought patterns. But that person is able to quickly deal with the issue at hand and proceed in creating their life. Mind mastery does not negate dealing with karma, or learning in duality – as long as we are here, it is a prerequisite. If you are experiencing frequent limitations and lack, this means you are not at that level yet, thus you must apply more vigilance to your feelings and thoughts, and be brave about examining what you are faced with.

When negative emotions occur, do not believe them to be "the truth" about the situation. Remember that it is you who generated these emotions and it is the current belief that you need to examine about how true it really is for you *now*. Suppressing negative emotions is not a solution, they fester and rot inside the emotional body, which then only destabilizes us further, and generates dis-ease in the physical body. Stored unprocessed (unfelt) emotions in the physical body only create blockages in the cellular systems and organs. Our matter body systems are like "highways" for the energy flow and if they are blocked, that system can stop functioning properly (autoimmune problems, allergies, atherosclerosis, nervous breakdown). Our organs are like "databases" for the unprocessed energy (in the brain we store confusion, in the sinuses – sadness, in the heart – loss and not-enoughness, in the liver – anger, in the pancreas – bitterness, in the kidneys – fear, etc.) All suppressed emotions "eat us" from the inside. For example, unprocessed anger directed outwards might mutate into bitterness, while if it is directed inwards, it will become guilt. Or the suppressed fear projected outwards will be felt as anything from anxiety to paranoia, and if pushed inwards, will become depression and not-enoughness. Unprocessed emotional reactions are "emotional toxin", and they only breed more issues for our system. Recognizing the feeling and accepting its existence in our energy system is necessary in order to re-program. Only then will we be able to gain Mind mastery, when we are consciously directing emotional responses, raising the quality of our lives.

Emotional triggers are stimuli, received through one or more of the five body senses. You could have heard something, seen something, tasted, smelled, or physically experienced something. Once the trigger has occurred, it takes three seconds for that information to travel to the brain, which then de-codes it according to our current attitude, as "good" or "bad". During these three seconds we can apply our Mind to the issue and by the time the impulse arrives into the brain, our emotional reaction will be the one we chose to have. These three seconds are the window of opportunity for Mind mastery to be applied. At first it is almost impossible to do it this fast. Once we are triggered, we feel the pre-programmed predictable emotional reaction right away. It feels instantaneous, but it is not.

How do you get good at using your Higher Mind during this three second window? First you must deal with the issues, and this means you will miss the three second window, and have a habitual emotional reaction. Then you must look at the thought and belief behind it, trace it to the origin and resolve the issue. Once you do this enough times, you will be able to link the stimuli to the proper "changed" concept. This means that when you receive familiar stimuli, you immediately are aware of the entire chain of events:

stimuli → emotional reaction → belief it is based on → a new more balanced belief it shall be replaced with. And so you are able, eventually, to go directly into the last position – the new balanced belief that you have decided shall be in the place of the old imbalanced one. Then right after the stimuli you already know which belief to focus on – this occurs immediately, within the three second window, and so the emotional reaction that follows is now based on your re-programmed conceptual understanding, not an old karmic belief.

Brain "Androgyny"

The material brain is a component of our path to Self Mastery. The spiritual component of human nature cannot be reduced to electrical and chemical processes in the physical brain. When our medical science mapped the brain, saying which areas correspond to which feelings, thoughts and actions, they did not take into account that the brain itself does not think, feel, or act. The brain is a "translation device" between the planetary and personal energy field, and material perception. When one has a thought, it is one's mental body that generates it. And it does not start there either, because no thought is just born randomly, all thoughts are based on concepts. Some of these concepts we have integrated as convictions/beliefs, and so they are habitual, which also means they produce habitual thoughts. Other concepts are unintegrated, something we are just "trying on" like a new outfit, which produces "stray" thoughts – the type that generates "where the hell did this come from?!" But either way, the concepts generate thoughts, which then resonate with particular areas of the brain, which then creates a neuron activity in that part of the brain. So it is true that some parts of the brain are *related* to speech, others to memory, others to motor functions, and if these areas are damaged, these abilities also become compromised. This damage in the brain will surely result in the damage of the action it was connected to because these neurons cannot respond anymore to the energy frequencies related to them. Sometimes the brain can adjust and use other areas to receive the same frequencies, and then the damage is minimal. If one is living consciously, then even if the brain is damaged, it can be regenerated by the intention of that person, because their identity is perceived as outside of the matter body, and because of this it remains in authority with the body. The reason one might have difficulty regenerating the brain, or any other organ for that matter, is simply because one believes oneself to be the body, and one's authority is damaged when the body is damaged.

We are all androgynous beings. No one contains only one polarity. As entities, as Souls, we are both, always. When we come into form, we can assume more of one polarity to explore than another, depending on the atomic structure of our material form.

There are two types of particles that comprise all material things in this Universe. The two types are known as *bosons* and *fermions*, and their interactions define/describe all physical forms. The whole scheme of quantum field theory, for example, is that fermions interact by exchanging bosons. Fermions are electrons, muons, nutrinos, and quarks (the building blocks of matter – protons and neutrons); bosons are photons, gluons, Higgs bosons and gravitons. The two types of particles have fundamentally different natures: bosons are gregarious, and fermions are solitary. The solitary property of fermions leads to all chemistry and structure in general. For example, the pressure that stabilizes white dwarf and neutron stars is a result of fermions resisting further compression towards each other. No two fermions of the same kind can stand one another; they have to occupy different quantum states. In a way, it is similar to the repulsion between even polarities of a magnet; you can keep them together only if they are odd. This is also the reason why attempts to go through solid matter results in a serious injury on behalf of the brave volunteer ☺ (Only when we understand the consciousness of constituents of matter, does our perception expands beyond this "simulated limitation"). Fermions are the skeletal framework of things; bosons are what bind them together. Bosons may overlap in the same quantum state, and in fact the more bosons that are in a state the more likely that still more will join. Boson particles have no reason to repel one another and they bunch up into tight clusters.

The nucleus of an atom can be a fermion or boson depending on whether the total number of its protons and neutrons is odd (for fermion) or even (for boson).

Every complex form has both types. The human body is a complex form, and it is made of both fermions and bosons, but we naturally have more of one than the other type, which automatically makes us inclined more towards one polarity or the other – gregarious/ fluid/ merged or solitary/ structural/ individualized. As an entity, each of us has a harmonious balance of both, and we can be more structural in one lifetime, and more fluid in another. Sometimes Souls alternate their polarities in lifetimes, or prefer to stick to one polarity for many incarnations. We choose polarity for the body according to the lessons we need to learn in that lifetime.

The polarity of our personality in form, translated through brain development, is not based on the sex of the body!!! Instead it is based on the initial atomic makeup of the form we chose to incarnate into. Human society deliberately cultivates *rigid roles* for men and women (physical sexes), which suit **current** social beliefs.

130

In a patriarchal society males are taught to express competitiveness, assertiveness, courage, and leadership. Females are taught to express submissiveness and nurturing aspects, related to motherhood and nature. Children are raised by the mothers and taught by the fathers.

In a matriarchal society males are encouraged to express their physical prowess, but restricted in decision making. Females are taught to express wisdom in political and economical decisions. Children are raised by both parents, and taught by the mothers.

Neither social structure is fully harmonious, both will develop issues because of their rigidity. A harmonious social structure only arises when the individuality of each entity regardless of physical sex is respected and honored, and the wisdom is taught by anyone who has it, older members of society and children alike.

When a person is living unconsciously, which one of the internal polarities expressed is usually determined by social rules and cultural teachings (environment, family, and peer's expectations). Occasionally a Soul decides to activate a polarity that is not socially supported, which creates adversity and pressure – a difficult lesson, but capable of moving that entity along the journey faster. This is why male and female bodies do not always correlate with the fermionic or bosonic makeup. For example, someone in a female body can be more fermionic (more "male") but because society demands her to be "submissive and nurturing", experience significant self-worth issues (not being able to live a fully "female" role even if she tries). Or someone in a male body can be more bosonic and feel much more deeply than most men around him, and so be the subject of ridicule.

Depending on the atomic polarity, a human being develops one side of the brain more than the other. When one uses the left or logical hemisphere more, one is being analytical, attentive, objective and rational, able to process language, facts, science, math and strategies. The right hemisphere is driven by feelings, beliefs, imagination and subjective thinking. It is creative, impulsive, intuitive, caring and processes visually and multi-tasks. This of course determines the personality.

It is important to improve the less-dominant side of our brain, making both equally available to us.

Left brain support:

1- structuring a sentence with precision, perfecting spelling and grammar;
2- Logic-fuelled activities such as crosswords, Sudoku, math problems or a game of chess;
3- organizing data, making to-do lists and daily plans;
4- learning a new skill, activity or language.
5- READ that book, don't skim. Reading engages your mind wonderfully while skimming content and running your eyes through a page only weakens the left brain in the long run.

Right brain support:

1- take five minutes off to observe your desk, your kitchen, your closet. Remember the details with your eyes closed. Doing this regularly will strengthen your powers of observation and your memory.
2- Play word association, doodling and memory games to support your creativity.
3- Do art – sketch, paint, dance, perform, write creatively – anything that does not require you to learn, do it as a child would, fully believing that you can (you can always throw it away later if you do not like it).

4- Play an instrument that is easy and does not require lots of structural learning. Sing, and while humming to your favorite tunes, make up random lyrics that rhyme.
5- Visualize and immediately implement these steps.
6- Play sports like golf, tennis and badminton.

In western society, the left brain is respected and advanced. People who can think, strategize and act decisively are rewarded. In eastern traditions the right brain is honored. The ones who are creative, imaginative and open to flow have the best experience. Without intuition, inspiration, and inner guidance from the right brain, choice and creativity cannot happen. And the other way around, without planning, strategizing, sustained effort and the focused responsibility of the left brain, freedom and mastery cannot occur. We need both hemispheres of our brains to work in order to enter harmony.

Right now most people have one side of the brain functioning, while the other does not. Making both sides work at peak efficiency is already a good goal. But we can take it one step further – they can work together as ONE. This is possible through the "neurobiology of Unity" – the corpus callosum, a thick bundle of 200 million nerve fibers that forms a communication network between the left and right hemispheres of the brain. The corpus callosum is an underutilized structure that enables creative thought and unites logic with irrationality. As we progress on the path of Self Mastery, we attain brain synchronization. This means that each of the hemispheres are not only able to function well when needed, but are also communicating with one another, working as one unit. Brainwave entrainment produces hemispheric synchronization. By creating hemispheric synchronization, entrainment can lead to greater intellectual functioning of the brain. Electrical stimulation, motion systems, acoustic field generators and even isolation tanks can increase hemispheric symmetry of the brain. Utilizing affirmations and deep states of meditation are ways of connecting to the "middle path" (out of duality), which allows the brain to function as a unified mechanism, that further expands the perceptional range of the brain "owner".

The universe rearranges itself to accommodate our model of reality. The Spirit part of us, the Divine Self (the "I AM"), radiates to the Divine Mind, which further radiates into the cellular body. In order for us to be self-aware individuals, to comprehend our uniqueness and experience it consciously, we use our linear mind here, in the linear time dimension of perception. Our linear mind is the lower mind, concerned with survival strategies. When we are disconnected in our self-perception from the Higher Mind, we are also disconnected from the Divine Self of Spirit. Here the lower mind programs our emotions, which then negatively affect our body.

Stepping into the awakening of Self requires an expansion of self-perception to Divine Mind and Divine Self. We achieve Divine Mind alignment by mind-mastery and knowing, and through it we can consciously program ourselves. We arrive into the "I Am" state of Self through detachment and being-ness, by means of which we can affirm the higher truth.

This process cannot be hurried, for it does not activate until one is ready, and that is determined by the experiences that the entity has had. It would not be correct for everyone to suddenly begin to have an interest in spiritual matters. Many are in the steps of creating initial self-awareness, and so these entities will have to go through survival patterns for mastering that.

Our planet has the most diverse range of self-awareness: from "nursery" and "kindergarten" (animalistic, survival of the fittest, sexual competition) to the various school grades (emotional, intellectual, behavioral and religious competition), to the "college" level (seeing/understanding of how life works, asking big "why?" questions), "master school" level (internal spirituality, seeing patterns in reality) and "graduate school" level (practicing conscious living, and various levels of awakening).

As you probably guessed, on this planet there are many people on the basic levels of consciousness (who occasionally resist learning altogether, which then is "corrected" by their Soul attracting to them experiences which motivate them to move again), and very few the further up we go. It is the way of things and it is all in perfect order. When the Soul stirs inside, one begins to desire knowledge that will take one on the path of self-discovery. He/she honors the intellect by researching spiritual materials already available on the planet, soon recognizing that all world religions and ancient mystery schools have common threads of higher truth in their origins. One studies biology, quantum physics, cosmology, symbology, mythology, interconnectedness of nature, ecology, and the energy system. One learns to let go of a particular religious or scientific path as the "only way", and instead chooses among many the path that is the most suited for him/her personally. One discovers the Universal Laws of creation and understands how to work within them to create the life that one desires. One practices, plays and creates magic inside their life perception.

Intentions and Manifestation

Intent is a *purposeful aligned design*. Affirmations and self-programing are ways of intent-application in order to manifest a desired reality. *Affirmation* is a *strong declaration*. **Programming** is a *sequence of command instructions* from the Higher Mind. The Higher Mind then influences the lower mind, the emotional body and the physical body, manifesting what we desire. Manifesting our desires is guaranteed. But this guarantee has six "small print" clauses:

1- *embodying the truth that "I Am God"* (for affirmations) and *alignment with the Divine Mind* (for self-programing);
2- alignment with the perfect *"Universal Timing"*;
3- *precise* wording;
4- faith/ belief without proof;
5- detachment;
6- *absence of doubt* (facing/consciously transmuting the "internal Saboteur").

And these six parameters are often the reasons why intentions do not work. Making a positive affirmation while having fears, worries, doubts and disbelief will achieve nothing. The same result will follow if an affirmation/intention is not continuous because we expected it to work immediately. If one is not detached while affirming (i.e. "know that it is"), it is very easy to manifest the fears of not getting what we want instead. If one does not comprehend, agree and embody as personal truth the knowledge that we are all interconnected, that our thoughts generate our perceptions and that there are Universal Laws that govern energy interactions, NO affirmation will work because its origin will be "too low" (instead of originating in one's Divine Self, it will emanate from the lower mind).

One's __attention__ to the emotion, and subsequently the thought/belief that generated it, invites its vibration into one's experience.

This works regardless if you like the emotion/thought or not! When you desire to experience something and you focus on it, you vibrate at the rate of that emotion/thought, i.e. you attract it into your personal experience. When you feel an intense dislike of something, through emotions of fear or pain, you are vibrating at the rate of that dislike, i.e. you are inviting that very undesirable thing into your personal experience.

This is why detachment is necessary for awakening. It allows us to release unconscious intense emotions, so we stop bringing these unwanted experiences into our lives. When detachment is mastered, intent is under our conscious command, and so is the application of intense desire upon request of our Higher Selves.

Detachment does not mean "no desires," instead it implies the knowing that any desire that is in alignment with the Universe is __already fulfilled__.

Our brains form neural networks based on our experiences. The environment and triggers of this life influence the brain, they also awaken the karmic patterns existent in the emotional body, which then imprint upon the brain. During our childhood years, the brain is learning to perceive this material reality as "real". You might even remember that when you were a young child, you saw reality in different terms, more fluid and moldable, less solid and definite. This is because as children we all are closer to the Divine Self than adults. As the body grows, we gradually become hard-wired by growing neural response patterns to support the communal perception of materiality.

By the age of seven, the brain is programmed with accepted neural networks, and overlaid with major karmic ones. Over the course of a lifetime, these neural networks are refined, new karmic ones are overlaid, activated by the triggers, pre-programmed into one's life. This automated refinement of the neural patterns can be modified by conscious self-programming.

Programming is repetition of a specific request until the new neural patterns have been formed, which then provides the construction of reality of what was desired. This process is never instant, but some results can be felt right away. Programming requires extremely precise wording. Since the result of programming mirrors the intent, the specificity is everything. Negative terms should never be used because our subconscious mind will focus on these instead of the meaning we are implying (subconscious mind is very literal). It is also essential that we are very certain about what we wish to create – overly vague and/or directionless statements will bring no results. For example, instead of "I never doubt myself" (firstly, your body will not believe "I never" because it knows you have had doubts in the past and they are stored in your cellular memory; secondly, the word "doubt" is negative; thirdly, which "myself" do you mean here?) say *"I choose to stand in certainty of my Divine Self"* (this sentence brings it to the current moment, has positive flavor and a clear instruction).

138

Our entire being is a broadcasting station, generating a particular resonance. When this resonance is congruent throughout the energy field and in alignment with the Divine Self, the Universe responds by rearranging itself to match our creative desire. Cellular memory sabotages the higher broadcasts if it disagrees with them, and in doing so sabotages manifestation of what the higher part of us desires. Allowing oneself to be run by accumulated cellular memory will keep one busy for many lifetimes! Through self-programing one essentially is able to re-program these incongruent cellular imprints. This frees one's intention from the interference of discordant energies.

Intent is a choice. To choose is to exercise the power of Divine Mind. One can choose to intend for a particular duration of linear time. Or one can program the intent as a "recurring program," supported by the spherical time of "I Am" Divine Self (*in my book "Mission Alpha" I call it the "always-intent-mode"*).

For example, your intent to manifest health when you are recovering from a cold, can be programmed for a week, while your intent for confidence might be set as a "recurring program" (an "always-intent-mode") for the rest of your life.

A *wish* is a form of desire, not intent. We intend to manifest what we desire, i.e. we program/affirm that our desire is already existent in our perception. Wishing implies lack, it is desire to have something we feel we do not have. Wishing affects only the Emotional and Astral bodies, while intent programs (holds in alignment and vibrates through) the structural bodies first, which in turn affect the fluid ones (Emotional and Astral).

If something we intended for did not materialize, we need to examine these six "small print" clauses to make sure we are on track:

1- Did the reasons for this intention originate high enough? (Did you intend for something because it was a more harmonious state of being, or was it out of avoidance of something you did not like?)
2- Were you ahead of yourself, not patient? (Your intention rang true in your system, but more work is required before you can fully embody it?)
3- Were your words messy and direction unclear? (Did you spend time thinking to find *precise* clear wording for your intent?)
4- Were you able to "believe without proof" or did you get scared as soon as the proof did not materialize right away?
5- Were you overly wrapped up in "having to make it happen" instead of detachment?
6- Did you investigate and neutralize your "internal saboteur"?

The #2 here is one of the hardest pieces because we do not always count on divine timing. The time delay between intention and manifestation is an opportunity to practice self-mastery, and learn nuances of alignment. This timing is Divine Will, it is a component of the bigger picture of events, the Divine Blueprint. It can be frustrating when you are in alignment, yet manifestation of your intent does not occur. This is because this Divine Blueprint consists of many puzzle pieces – events, people, awareness etc. Some events might not have occurred yet, some people might not have stepped into their roles yet, some awareness has not been revealed or acquired yet.

A useful program here might be *"I choose to clearly perceive the next piece of Divine Blueprint, and bring to me the perfect people and events that are instrumental in implementation of this Blueprint, so that it can physically manifest now."*

140

If you are having trouble with Divine Timing, applying **Feng Shui** (ancient Chinese system of geomancy that uses the energies of elements to improve life by attracting positive chi/prana/life force) could be of great benefit. The life area connected to the Northwest direction of your home is called "Helpful People & Blessings". It is important to amplify the energy flow to the Northwest area of your home, and to express your gratitude for all the helpful/beneficial energy already in your life. It is the ideal place for personal symbols of gratitude (pictures or objects). That area is ruled by the Metal element, so use metal objects and frames, white, gray and metallic colors, and everything vertical and tall (lamps, sculptures, narrow picture frames).

Intentions can easily be diffused by the "internal Saboteur", a belief or memory that is opposite from that which we are stating. This "Saboteur" is a secondary pattern that runs parallel to the one we are affirming, thus they cancel each other out.

One of the main "Saboteurs" to being in alignment with "I Am" Divine Self is the belief that we are only spiritual if we do "right, spiritual things", like meditate, or do lucid dreaming, or eat a certain way, take vitamins, and many other limiting ideas we subscribe to.

An example of intent (program) that can override this pre-set self-judgment is this: "*All my energy bodies, and my cellular body, are harmonious with the Universe. This is the truth in every moment, whether I eat, sleep, exercise, meditate or do anything else.*" By choosing to program yourself with this intent, you are transmuting limiting feelings and thoughts.

Self Care

It is impossible to properly use intent or arrive at a different level of self-awareness without a certain amount of self-knowledge and inner guidance, which can only be gained through spending some time alone. Unfortunately we are conditioned to serve others, like spouses, children, family, job, friends, but not ourselves. Yet what would happen to one's relationships if one stopped paying attention to them, stopped listening and taking them seriously? Our relationships would fall apart if we did not nourish them with our attention. Spending some time alone, without any external distractions, is the best way one can honor relationship with oneself. Half of this time must be devoted to self-education – reading books, studying, listening to inspirational broadcasts and so on. The other half must be spend in experiencing the Great Silence. It can be done by meditation or visualization, by taking a quiet walk through a garden or on a beach, through sitting and consciously focusing on yourself, talking through what has arisen in your life, listening to yourself, aligning with the Divine Self. Self-knowledge cannot be delivered to you from the outside. You can use many external materials to inspire you and show you what is possible, but the rest is up to your own personal investigation of yourself and the Universe around you.

No one can become enlightened while diminishing their own value in that the Light must awaken within. Spiritual Self-care is our main job while here in matter. Our awakening depends on it!

In the material area of our lives, self-care can be divided into four categories:

- water intake,
- food intake,
- movement,
- rest.

It is our responsibility to allow our matter-vehicles, our bodies, to function properly in these areas. Drinking a lot of water is necessary for hydration, for electro-magnetic conductivity of the energies we are processing, for the flushing out of toxins. Structured or pyramid-charged water is the best (*more on this in the "Structure Water" chapter, page152*).

As one journeys into awakening, one becomes ether-based, not water-based, and so eventually water is not necessary, but that can only occur after there is no need for material food either, so meanwhile – drink up!

We are what we eat, and so the food we send through our digestive tracts must be as pure as possible: organic and light. Red meat and sugar are the heaviest substances out there, followed by dairy products; chicken and eggs are lighter, fish and sea food even lighter, and vegetables, fruits and nuts are the lightest. No food change should be exercised based on mental or political decisions. Sometimes we actually need the substance we think we should not eat. Birch tree sugar (made from its juice) and strawberry sugar are a better option if sugar is still desired. But once the inner work is commencing there is a lot more clarity about which foods are right for you.

Everyone is different. When a person is feeling angry a lot, letting go of eating red meat would be a great choice, while if someone is experiencing much fear and anxiety, and inability to pay attention to material matters, they might actually benefit by adding some red meat into their diet for a while. When the inner work brings a person to a fast and light vibrational range, he might not have any desire anymore for heavy foods – they would serve no purpose in his body. At this stage, foods like vegetables, grains, nuts, fruits and honey would be the best. Honey is also sugar, but it is holographically harmonious with the planet, because the bees have added sacred geometry codes into the honey through a special enzyme which divides the sucrose into glucose and fructose – two simple sugars for our bodies to absorb directly, synchronizing us with the planet.

Eventually the amount of life force/prana one can receive increases so much that there is no more need for material food. But we cannot hurry that moment, because if the body is not ready to receive the required amount of etheric energy, yet we stop feeding it material food, it will essentially go on a diet, a fast, and that is a *deprivation*.

All diets are based on the "not-enoughness code", while living on etheric energy without material food is based on the "abundance code" - in living on energy there is more than enough food, only it has changed its state from physical to non-physical, from matter to energy.

Movement does not have to be strenuous exercise. When we are in the process of working through our fears and issues, we might require very active work-outs. Getting into the body and building relationship with it is necessary in order to help it awaken, and building muscle will definitely get you into the body! Very active aerobic exercise is affective in dispersal of fears and anxiety. But as one becomes more attuned to the higher vibrations, less strenuous exercise becomes more appropriate – like walking, yoga, Thai Chi, etc. Eventually breathing itself becomes all that the body needs. Deep breathing exercises not the muscles (the macrocosm) but the cells (microcosm). As the rate of vibration of the material body increases, it will not require oxygen either, being able to breathe the life force directly. Obviously do not try to do *that* until you are ready!

Rest is not only about sleep, it is about being calm and harmonious. When we are in stress and anxiety, in worry and circular thinking, we are not at rest! Intense energies are meant to activate our systems, but it is our responsibility to use the positive end of that energy. For example, if you are experiencing anxiety,

146

switch your inner viewpoint and it will become excitement. Frustration can become courage to face the issue, depression can become emotional letting go, confusion can turn into the experience of spaciousness and opening for something new to come in.

There is a common misconception that when one does the consciousness work, one needs less sleep. During sleep we recharge and regenerate the body, but we also download information, allow our "medical team" guides to help us with upgrades, process energy and, eventually do a lot of "travel" and energy work consciously. Therefore sleep is a tool we can use. Anyone on the path to enlightment knows that some days you need many hours of sleep, maybe for weeks, while other days no sleep comes at all. Sleep patterns change as we do our personal work – some sleep more than they used to, others less. When one does a lot of processing of energy (emotional, mental and physical) during the day, one might need to sleep more to process its effects in the body. If one is in very high frequency, one might not feel like sleeping at all (and as long as you are able to do this without feeling tired the next day – great, don't sleep!) On the other hand, one might have done work with very high vibration during the day, requesting answers, teachings, support – which might require much longer sleep, so as to receive these answers, teachings and support! Be kind to yourself, and never override your sleep patterns, allow them to unfold and use them appropriately.

For the emotional and astral bodies self-care is about detoxifying the past and letting go of trauma. The emotional body is meant to be in the moment, it cannot plan ahead. When it experiences emotion, it feels 100% real now, even if it is something that we are tuning into from the past, or something we are anticipating in the future. Thus it is our responsibility to make sure that these emotions are in support of our journey. Negative emotions need to be felt in order to be processed, but getting stuck in them is masochistic and unnecessary. One does not get any points for feeling guilty! Self-punishment is a learned response based on the idea that we are children requiring a parent – when a parent is unavailable, we do it to ourselves. Transmuting negative into positive in each moment creates a state of harmony in the emotional body.

Self-approval is also essential. For the Divine Self or the Higher Mind this concept of self-approval is irrelevant because being God implies existence, perfect in every moment. However while we are here in the material body, approval still plays an important role for most. Seeking approval from the external reality will only take one further away from their true Self. External approval negates inner guidance and takes the place of an internal navigator. By seeking approval from the outside we essentially state that someone else knows us better than we know ourselves. That is impossible, because true knowledge of Self can only come from within, although it can be supported by the external guidance and triggers.

The action of Self-approval is indeed self-congratulation!

When you do something well, succeed in handling a situation with consciousness, take the "higher road" in an argument, allow for self-care – congratulate yourself! Notice your achievements and support yourself on the path of awareness. Do so daily.

The Mental, Truth and Conceptual bodies' self-care is all about Mind Mastery. Monitoring and realigning the concepts, which generate the thoughts, leads to conscious creation.

Vigilance about our habitual thinking is also an essential component of self-care. Remember that everything we are feeling is always based on a particular thought process which comes out of a particular belief. If one is unhappy, it is one's responsibility to disengage from the external trigger for that unhappiness and search for the thoughts/beliefs which created it. I often hear people, overwhelmed with emotional reaction, say "but I am not thinking anything!" – that is just not true. The only reason one does not notice one's thoughts in that moment is because these thoughts are so habitual that one sees them as an "unquestionable reality".

Having a vision of Self is another important component of self-care. What we can *imagine* having we can *attract*. If one never investigates what one wants to become, many options are closed to them – one's broadcast is limited to the already known "stations". If you cannot believe something, it will not be possible. The absence of unlimited thinking is quite often the cause for one's stagnation. When our thinking patterns are limited, we circle over and over the same pathway, feeling trapped, unworthy, lost, purpose-less and insignificant. This is why it is essential to allow yourself time for envisioning yourself in an expanded way. Think in possibilities instead of impossibilities for every event, every moment. Give yourself permission to dream an amazing life into existence – imagine what you would like your life to be, and what can you do to create that, then feel your desire for that life rising powerfully inside you – hold that vision and amplify it by re-visiting it, elaborating on it. This way you create a direction for your life to unfold. It might end up looking exactly like what you have imagined, or different, but if you are not *"walking* on the path", life cannot help you!

Structured Water

Structured water is the water which is in harmony with the Universal Blueprint, it is the "water of Nature". If you pour water into a mountain stream at the top of the mountain and then collect it at the bottom, the water is structured. Structured water is free of memory. The main contingent in a molecule of structured water is life force energy. The water molecule has the power, the individual authority to uphold life, and that is to cleanse it from the things that are adverse to life and to generously provide the things that are good for life. Structured water's design looks like a snowflake; this is the most bioavailable (able to be absorbed by a biological organism) type of water for our bodies.

Structured water has a lower surface tension and better hydrating properties. It has smaller high energy clusters, instead of the large low energy water molecule clusters. When one structures water, one eliminates negative energy-memory patterns, and redefines the water's natural healthy energy pattern. Structured water allows us to imprint through the DNA and RNA the knowledge of the Divine Blueprint and help one to become balanced with the Universe.

Our physical bodies are 80% water. As we age, this percentage declines because our issues prevent the body from regenerating. The aging process involves a gradual loss of cell volume and an imbalance of the extracellular and intracellular fluids. This loss of cellular water can be accelerated when we don't ingest enough balanced liquids, or when our cell membranes aren't capable of maintaining a proper fluid balance. By drinking and washing our

150

bodies with structural water, we essentially reprogram the body. It is then able to release toxins (emotional and physical) faster, and regenerate better.

If you do not have easy access to a pure glacier, there are many ways to make structured water. Make-it-yourself options are: sincere heart-opening to the water, leaving water in a pyramidal structure for an hour, holding the glass with water in your hands and running pure White Light through it for at least ten minutes, and many more. You can also purchase a device that will allow your house water to run through it and structure it, restoring its original crystalline purity (I find that the most effective devices do not use any moving parts or electricity, but function by either allowing the water to move through a sequential path, which acts like a "compressed waterfall," or nano-programming).

Toning

Sound is a physicalized vibration, and vibrations which are within our material range realign vibratory patterns in matter-based forms. Toning is an intuitive fine tuning of the instrument that is our form. This applies to all our bodies: physical, Emotional, Mental and the rest. Toning can be used for helping blocked energy move, and for harmonizing. Toning is a fluid/female/magnetic way of working with energy. The good thing about toning is that one does not need to know what to do! One only needs to allow the sound, to let the universal consciousness work through one.

How to tone properly? One must begin with the note that matches the frequency of what one wants to work with – physical pain or issue, emotional pain, mental stuck-ness, spiritual lost-ness – whatever it is, the first note must match that energy. Once the first note is made, one must allow the next note to come – it cannot be reached by will or mental knowing – it has to "sound you" instead of you "sounding it". The tone will evolve from the painful initial note to the others, often many, as the energy unravels. It might sound very beautiful and harmonious, like a melody, or it might sound horrible. But one must persevere in trusting the tones to find their way back to harmony and allow their body to keep making sounds. Eventually even the most disharmonious sound will become balanced.

Toning can also be used to <u>raise one's frequency</u>. Intuitive toning of this type must begin with the most harmonious tone one can make (which means prior to making that note one must spend some time centering and calming). That initial note will sound through and must be allowed to keep going. You might notice that when you need to take a breath and the next note comes, it is the same – for a while. That is because this was the highest frequency that you could tune into, but not all of your own system was attuned to that frequency. When all of your bodies match the tone you are making, the next tone will naturally emerge, then the next, as you are upgrading your range. When using toning in this matter, you might notice that there are many energy guides who are participating with you, supporting the faster frequencies and helping you move up the tones.

A slightly more male/electric/structural way of using toning is the use of mantras. Mantras are sets of sound patterns, coded with particular thought-forms, and the feeling states they are meant to elicit. The code in these mantras is a compressed knowing, downloaded directly from the Divine Mind of the Universe. Although the term "mantra" is from India, most ancient cultures had some sound codes like that, and they usually imbedded them in the names of their holy beings, places, and sensory states. Even letters themselves can be mantras, if they are of high enough frequency to hold an entire program. The higher the frequency of the mantra code, the more access it will bring to the one experiencing it – it opens up one's connection with the Divine Mind. People of a more emotional type might experience that as a state of bliss, although bliss is simply a side-effect of being in the proper harmonious code. Mantras initial use was to help the knowing to expand, to help one become a more potent Self. As humankind went through the ages of "forgetfulness", mantras remained in use because of that nice side effect – unable to activate the knowledge, people were still harmonizing with the Light/Word/Code through the addiction to bliss...

Mantras are not simply sounded and/or heard, mantras are meant to be *experienced*. They are a full program, i.e. they are meant to realign the entire energy system, all of the bodies we have. And so sounding and hearing a mantra is meant to be a full system experience – only then will it have the full potential of opening the knowing. Unfortunately most people tune into the mantras through their mental level alone (which really has no beneficial result at all), or through their emotional body (which has a result of "feeling great", but does absolutely nothing for the Divine Mind).

All true mantras are related to Spirit. They resonate one way or the other with "Spirit is All That Is", and the converse proposition that "All That Is *is* Spirit"; and since a human being is included in the "all", we are resonating with the original description of a human being as the "likeness of God", which represents the fractal of the Universal hologram of Spirit.

Here are a few examples of high frequency mantras:

- "AUM" (it is the proper sounding of the "Om" mantra) is the trinity of the Cosmic Root Substance, the Creator, and the Light/Word/Code. When that sound is made, it synchronizes the resonance of one's energy field and physical body with the Universal Spirit.

- "*I Am That I Am*" is another sound conceptual code connected with this trinity, vibrating the individual Self in resonance with the Universal Spirit.

- "*Nuk-Pu-Nuk*" is an ancient Egyptian mantra that means "I Am who I Am". It was recorded on the walls of ancient temples, and chanted especially in On, the City of Light (which Greeks later called Heliopolis, the City of the Sun). The ancient Egyptian city of On is the place from where Moses, who was raised as a son of a pharaoh's daughter and highly educated in Egyptian teachings, borrowed the explanation for the Hebrew god Jehovah/Yahve (YHWH).

- "*Yod-hay-vod-hay*" (YHVH) is a Jewish chant, representing non-duality/androgyny of Self (the unity of the feminine and masculine).

- "*Allahu Akbar*" means "The Sole Deity is Great", it was originally meant as a <u>celebration of the Spirit Most High</u>. In pre-Islamic Arabia, Meccans used the term Allah as a name for the Supreme Creator Deity. Allah was considered the Creator of the World, and had angels/jin associated with him, and his offspring as all other gods.

- *"Om Mane Padme Hum"* is a Sanskrit mantra, associated with the Bodhisattva of Compassion. As the 14th Dalai Lama explains: "These six syllables mean that in dependence on the practice of a path which is an indivisible union of method and wisdom, you can transform your impure body, speech, and mind into the pure exalted body, speech, and mind of a Buddha". To simplify, "om" symbolizes impure body transmuted into pure, "mane" means "jewel", indicting a path of altruistic intention to become enlightened, while "padme" means "lotus", indicating wisdom, and "hum", as a conclusion (jewel/intent + lotus/wisdom) indicates indivisibility of Spirit.

- *"Kadoish, Kadoish, Kadoish, Adonai Tseybeyoth"* is a very powerful mantra because it represent the ascension process of this Universe. Kadoish means holy, Adonai means the Master (often mistranslated as Lord), and Tseybeyoth (Sabaoth for Gnostics in Coptic Christianity) is the name of the forces of Light. In Gnostism (from Nag Hammadi scrolls) Sabaoth is the opposite to Yaldeboath, who is the arrogant creator, attempting to override Spirit, while Sabaoth represents the harmonious-with-spirit-creation. This mantra is often translated as "Holy, Holy, Holy Lord's Armies" and used as a protection mantra (it does resonate with the highest Light and thus repel anything of disharmony), although the more balanced way of looking at it would probably be "Sacred Master of force of Light". This mantra is Ugaritic-Sumerian-Hebrew in origin, one of the most ancient mantras. It is the Code for the Universal Hologram, which synchronizes oneself with the Divine Mind. Sounding this mantra must be done three times in a row for the best effect. It unifies both hemispheres of the brain and facilitates clarity, focus and discernment.

Morphogenic Fields

Morphogenesis is an initiation into form, the coming into being as form.

In developmental biology, a morphogenetic field is a group of cells able to respond to discrete, localized biochemical signals, leading to the development of specific morphological structures/organs. Within the morphogenic field there exists a collection of interacting cells out of which a particular organ is formed. As a group, the cells within a given morphogenetic field, are constrained. However, the specific cellular programming of individual cells in a field is flexible: an individual cell can be redirected via cell-to-cell signaling to replace specific damaged or missing cells elsewhere.

Morphogenic (or Morphogenetic) fields are electro-magnetic templates/blueprints, created by everything in existence; it is the input and output of creation. They are created by planets, by the Sun, by Nature, by diverse energy entities and by us. With every intense feeling/emotion, thought and action (or non-action) every individual strengthens one of these fields that are already in existence. Some of these fields are lower-astral monstrosities of hatred and fear, while others are amazing healing and nurturing blueprints of peace and beauty. With the clear intention to channel a feeling, and/or with the focus of enough minds, we can create/support a new morphogenic field – of peace, responsibility and Self-consciousness (Unity-consciousness).

The current level of human consciousness is the "training wheels" stage for the formation of Self. It has created many morphogenic fields separate from Nature, not based on beneficial planetary instinctual intelligence. The dominant consciousness ("mass consciousness") on the planet right now is fear-based, as it has formed from the negative sense of separation, scarcity and war. Our "mass consciousness" is disharmonic because it includes the actions, thoughts and feelings of humans who are locked inside of the image projections of what a self should be, instead of the true Self. At the same time that our mass consciousness is fear-based, there are other morphogenic fields that exist based on peace, healing, beauty, and love. <u>All morphogenic fields in existence change their field strength with every individual feeling, thought, and action that occurs.</u>

All matter-species (human beings, animals, plants, crystals/minerals) and all non-matter species, have a consciousness and therefore relate to a particular morphogenic field. The energy connected to an emotion/feeling is one of the most powerful forces of creation of morphgenic fields for humans, although as we evolve, we will be able to use this energy in combination with clear focused thought. A large number of people simultaneously focusing on a particular feeling or thought will generate a local morphogenic field (there are many "internet intention-setting opportunities" floating around, when people circulate a desire for a particular intent setting at a particular time, so that everyone who

158

chooses to participate adds their intent in the pre-set moment, and they have resulted in creations of scattered balanced peaceful morphogenic fields on Earth). For this to be accomplished on a planetary scale, 22% of humanity has to hold that same feeling/emotion. With enough input, the morphogenic field itself creates a ripple effect that people, knowingly or unknowingly, are able to tap into.

Embracing our collective responsibility to achieve a level of personal transformation will impact our collective morphogenetic field. Transformation on this collective level is vital for sustainable enlightenment and continuing conscious evolution on both personal and planetary scales.

Individually and collectively we constantly contribute to the development of our Universe with our thoughts and the emotional content behind them. This is why awakening to the next level of consciousness cannot be possible without responsibility – not only for our actions, but also for our internal environment – thoughts, feelings, senses.

Morphogenic fields are accessed by generating a particular resonance to match the field's frequency, (fear attracts more fear; anger amplifies anger; compassion brings compassion). Because higher frequencies are more harmonious, high frequency morphogenic fields can modify/heal lower frequency ones: a field of compassion will resolve hatred; a field of love will resolve war (these are usually the intents of the internet-based intention-setting morphogenic fields).

One is able to connect to a morphogenic field at any moment from anywhere – all one needs is an ability to resonate at a particular frequency. Morphogenic fields are an amazing tool for training our consciousness to expand, and for releasing limited patterns.

This is how you can practice:

1- pick a particular issue that you want to work on (self-hatred, confusion, fear, anger, insecurity, scarcity, etc.)
2- tune into how this issue manifests in your energy field and body, where you feel it the most;
3- once you can experience the issue in your system, look for the morphogenic field that it is linked to (any issue of fear is linked to the planetary astral fear field; the issue of scarcity to the planetary field of human-generated scarcity, etc.)
4- notice how much of the issue is your own and how much is being supported/maintained by the planetary morphogenic field (in % maybe?);
5- tune into the morphogenic field of a higher frequency than the one you are linked to, a field that would dissolve your link to the lower field (i.e. tune into the field of uniqueness if you were dealing with insecurity; or to the field of love if you are dealing with hatred; or to the field of purpose if you are dealing with lost-ness, and so on.)
6- witness how linking to the morphgenic field of higher frequency dissolves the link to the lower field. Now you are left with only your own issue, without the negative support of the lower field. We are designed to work with our own issues and they are much easier to handle when they do not link up with everyone else's! By doing this you just made your own issue more manageable and at the same time released your support of human negativity, helping others do the same.

Genetic Hologram

The Earth is constantly generating density patterns, which allow for material life to exits. But if our DNA is not in the divine state, we ourselves risk generating more exponentially intensifying density waves. This keeps us in a negative state, stuck *in between* balanced instinctual/animal consciousness and balanced realized-Self consciousness.

To access the divine DNA state, we each need to choose living the qualities of an ascended being, one step at a time...

The Source is constantly radiating life force activation streams through all of Creation. Photonic Light codes imbedded in these streams are an informational feeding of Spirit/Source consciousness. They are geometrically patterned to stimulate and upgrade our DNA codes. Our evolutionary symbiotic relationship with the Source, the Earth, the Sun and every planet within the original design of our Solar System, and with each other, is dependent on these codes.

Our ability to access these codes, and harmonically recalibrate with these cosmic influences, is reliant on our proficiency to receive, translate and utilize Light/Word/Code. We are continually exchanging data flows with Source intelligence/Spirit and the body of Earth. These circuits of electro-magnetic exchange join us together – One Life, one matrix of co-creative space-time, the unified field consisting of multitudes of morphogenic templates.

If we can relax, be enough, take time for appreciating life, find pleasure in the smallest of experiences, and *risk* in order to grow, then we will enhance our receptivity to Light/Word/Code.

The amalgamation of millions of visible and invisible systems generates the human hologram. We are multidimensional codes ourselves, radiating/broadcasting frequencies of our consciousness to the Universe. The primary system that supplies this hologram with creative intelligence is the DNA-generated matter-vehicle (our physical bodies are acting like broadcast stations).

The highest spiritual imprint is imbedded in the human matrix. It is built on the vibratory infrastructure of energy pathways that follow geometric patterns (the etheric DNA codes). These further vibrate into density, generating material DNA. After the advancement to the next level of consciousness we cease being materially based, thus the further level codes are stored in the etheric DNA only.

Conscious communion with sacred geometry is an intrinsic component in the reactivation of the divine "immortal" DNA blueprint. Sacred geometric forms emit a frequency, in search of a like frequency with which to resonate that communes with the vibratory infrastructure of our perfect DNA blueprint. Through this resonance the structural integrity of the original human template is reinforced.

Our DNA is consciousness crystallized into form. This crystalline structure exists etherically as well as materially. The divine "immortal" human blueprint is linked to Unity Consciousness ("Vertical Belonging") and holds the integrity of the true etheric DNA matrix. The blueprint is in synergy with the vibratory infrastructure of our dormant DNA because it is built upon the laws of resonant harmonics. In other words, *our bodies will wake us up if we allow it!* As we reconnect our electro-magnetic, biologically based systems to the sacred geometric forms, we activate the dormant codes. The geometry, the language of Light, is the key that opens the door, and then the Love of Spirit/Source pours in.

This "upgrade" of energy activates the brain and revitalizes the endocrine system. This allows us to receive, decode and utilize the geometries of Light/Word/Code. As we proceed individually on this path, we may collectively stabilize a new model of existence, a paradigm resonant with the integrity of Light.

Releasing Tribal Consciousness

Humanity in general is moving from the negative Tribal Consciousness *("me vs. you")* to the balanced Unity Consciousness *("One Life")*. This is a hard transition for many people because their identities are linked to the tribe that they feel they belong to, just as their pains are linked to the tribes that they felt they were abandoned by or pushed out of (circle of friends, family, country, religion/church, job). In the "tribal" way of living the "right-ness" of that tribe becomes the rule, which perpetuates wars with other tribes, each believing in their "right-ness". Imagine two rams, horns locked, pushing at one another. One wins an inch, then another, but all in all they remain pretty much locked in the same position. This is what human cultures have experienced on this planet for a very long time, in every area of life: politically, religiously, socially, medically, and even internally!

The release of this "tribal right-ness" is a necessary component in becoming a Divine Self, aligned with Divine Mind. Each person is responsible for the release of their own tribal mentality. This of course does not mean that humans suddenly will agree on everything. But by choosing "tolerant individuality" we are moving from *competition* to *cooperation and complementarity*. Competition as a way of progress only works on the beginning stages of self-awareness. Once a person initiates curiosity about the higher dimensions of Self, competition becomes irrelevant. Transcendence of duality is the ultimate goal of internal Personal Alchemy. By the means of "tolerant individuality" we are returning to the immortal state of being.

Matter and Spirit are one energy in different stages of manifestation. These stages allow for alternate ways in which we perceive ourselves and our reality.

This level of perception (this morphogenic field of one energy) is the recognition of the holographic nature of reality/manifestation. Through the comprehension of this holographic awareness we can appreciate deep levels of symbiotic resonance that define us as individualized aspects (Selves) of the unified divine consciousness (Spirit/Source).

Our physicality is a complex manifestation of our divinity, individualized by our wisdom and by our karma.

We are designed to be everlasting – we are held in the matrix of the Universe as precious vehicles for enriching the Spirit/Source. Our human DNA is uniquely designed for this task. The masterpiece of human design is the sensory organ for planetary ascension, as Earth is a sensory organ for human ascension. Our matter-form is a sacred geometric matrix, an instrument through which we will transcend this materialistic perception, entering into Unity Consciousness.

Our consciousness affects our chemistry, and vice versa. The disharmonious (dense) "tribal state" (consciousness) closed many divine codes in our DNA (chemistry). This state of DNA relates directly to our creations: disease, wars, genocide, cruelty, suffering. The mutations of our DNA codes are necessary for the learning curve. These DNA codes affect the translation of the holographic matrix of Light/Word/Code, which mirrors a state of collective unconsciousness back to us (sensory, visual and audio feedback).

One of the ways to remember the codes we came to Earth with, the codes originating from the time when we were ethereal entities of pure Light/Word/Code, before humans existed in matter-form, is by resonating with Nature. This is the original Unity Consciousness (the "Vertical Belonging") that we now are enhancing with individuality. Being able to relate to all life, feel its support and connectedness, while holding one's own uniqueness, reduces one's sense of isolation and separation.

Channeling as a Form of Communication

An alignment to the higher frequencies increases one's spiritual growth many times over, thus practicing that alignment is essential for awakening. The more we strengthen the inner connection to the Source within, the more purposeful and joyous our lives become.

Channeling is a way of aligning with the higher frequencies. All cultures trained and cherished individuals, who were able to communicate with the unseen, able to bring vision and purpose to their people. There are many names for these people – prophets, seers, shamans, oracles, mediums, psychics, channels. Some were born with an innate ability to remain in alignment, others had that ability activated by their own Soul, or through special training. There are three types of channels: trance channel, download channel, and conscious channel. The trance channel is a person who falls into an unconscious state to allow the information to come through – his everyday consciousness is unable to expand to the level where the information is coming from, therefore he "moves out of the way" (Edgar Cayce is a good example). Mediums are also examples of a trance channel – a medium is a person who not only "moves out of the way" energetically, but vacates his body altogether to allow another entity to enter and speak, using his material body. Download channel is a person who receives an entire package of information while being in an aligned state, but is unable to comprehend the information. In such case the information then has to be either tuned into for intuitive interpretation, or the knowing just "drops in" as the crown chakra translates it. The conscious channeling is only possible when one is

166

able to consciously not only uphold the alignment and travel along the vertical link established, but also able to fully comprehend the Code/information directly.

In all three versions of channeling, the source of the information varies. The message can be coming from the Higher Self/Soul, our personal energy guides, other entities/intelligences from other dimensions and/or time, and others. To complicate things, this information can arrive in many different forms: as a voice in one's mind, as a visual image, as a movie playing in one's mind, as a concept, or even something that moves the body (like making a sign, or writing, or drawing the information). Telepathic, verbal, auditory or written, the message still only has value for our awakening if it comes from a harmonious place in higher frequencies. Desiring a channeling ability for the reason of "feeling special" is caused by Lower Self insecurity and personal insignificance fears, and attracts entities from much lower frequencies which are less harmonious.

The channeled information is only as pure as the one receiving it, because the frequency range one can access is in direct proportion to one's own range. If someone only sees in black and white, but the information is in yellow, it cannot be delivered. This is why we can never receive answers out of desperation – desperation implies limitation in range of perception, it is always a wall that we must first face, before we can overcome it.

If one has done some inner work in their current and/or other lives and is able to align oneself with the higher vibrational component of oneself, that person will be able to download information within that range. That information might be from an external source, like a guide, or from one's Higher Self and will feel as if it has come from someone else – that is because that person has not expanded his own consciousness to incorporate this range into his own identity. And that information will be unknown by that person's conscious mind, it will feel external to it. Only if the conscious Self can expand to incorporate the range of frequencies will the information be known as one's own, or can be received in complete conscious communication with a guide or another entity.

How do you know what/who you are receiving the information from? All the beings who are interested in your awakening are resonant with service, inspiration, joy, and they are communicating with you not to simply "make you feel better", but to empower you, to give you tools you require, to support you on your journey. Information that is rigid, dualistic, judgmental, jealous, negative or disempowering of your journey comes from the entities who are interested in control and manipulation (the Yaldeboath kind – Gnostic's "arrogant creator"), or from your own fears. If, while attempting to practice channeling, you receive negative messages, it simply means you are not in alignment with the Source, the I Am That I Am presence of Spirit. If one assumes that someone outside of himself will fix his life, or change the events he himself is unable to, then one only gives his power away, and willingly! Just like in material life we have people who are kind and loving, helpful, and also people who are cruel and manipulative, honest people, and also judgmental and duplicitous people, and even people who mean well but end up not really helping... The same goes for the non-physical world. There are entities of the Sabaoth kind (Gnostic's "force of Light") who wish nothing but awakening for us, they work in harmony with the Cosmic Root Substance of Spirit, they are compassionate and kind, but they will never rescue us, because that would mean they took away our power, which goes against the overall plan of awakening! But there are also entities of the Yaldeboath kind who want the power that comes from Spirit, and since we humans are made by Spirit (and the Sabaoth kind), the Yaldeboath kind wants our energy. This means that occasionally they pretend to lead one into awakenings, but in reality they only lead to disempowerment (i.e. they get one's power). This does not mean that we must be afraid and use all sorts of protection spells to keep safe! If we do that, we fall into a very limited range of frequencies and become more susceptible to the manipulation, not less. Remember that we attract what we broadcast, so <u>if one wants to remain in the Sabaoth kind range, one must remain in self-awareness, love, kindness, compassion, absence of fear as a result of knowledge that all is One and nothing can ever harm one</u> (even Yaldeboath, although they do not know it!) – <u>everything is Spirit</u>.

I believe that the only guidance one can trust is the one gotten through one's inner teacher – the Higher Self, the Soul. The more one focuses on strengthening the connection with their own Higher Self (instead of anyone else out there that they might believe knows more about them), the better off they will be. Knowing our own Higher Self leads to two things: 1- clarity of Divine Mind becomes available to us; 2- the range of Self expands which means that the Higher Self and the Ego unite, and become a parent to the Lower Self, so it can be loved and eventually transmuted.

When one attempts to channel their own personal guides, two things occur: 1- one must raise their own range of frequencies, i.e. enter into an alignment with the highest energies one can master at the time; 2- the guide will lower its' range to the lowest possible point to attempt the overlap with the person in order to communicate. The guide will create an energy field in its dimension to resonate with the energy field of the person. It is very rare when a person has an exact energy match – that would mean

169

that the ranges are already overlapping. This tends to happen more often with the Souls that we have past life connections with, and occasionally, once one's work is done, with one's own Higher Self. If this is the case with a guide, then the channeling event would feel to you more like a regular conversation, only that it is going on in your mind.

The practice of aligning with one's Higher Self is the most important. The guides will do anything they can on their end to align to our current state. Most information is received through the right hemisphere of the brain, then analyzed/translated through the left, so it can come out as linear information, comprehensible to us down here in duality. As this occurs, new neuron patterns are being established (often resulting at first in intense headaches until the brain gets used to it), eventually leading to a whole new neuron map of the brain, which allows more ease in multidimensional communication. Practice makes perfect ☺

At first attempts at channeling it might feel to you as if you are just using your imagination. I suggest you try non-verbal forms of communication. If you have a question in mind, hold it there and await the answer. When you are in alignment, the answer you receive will feel like it did not come from your own mental body – i.e. you did not analyze the situation and arrive at this answer, instead the answer just showed up in your awareness. If you have difficulty shutting down your mental level, then use it first, analyze your own question and arrive at an answer, then ask again, and see what you receive. It might be a confirmation of your own conclusion or something totally different.

Perpetual Regeneration

We are eternal entities of pure energy who exist outside of linear time. There is no death of anything, only changes from one state to the next. The Soul cannot cease to exist – it is not possible to "lose your Soul", or "sell you Soul". You *are* the Soul! Souls design forms to experience existence inside the range of vibration for which the form was created. Each form is essentially a vibratory parameter. And the Soul is meant to have control within that parameter – this is Mastery. When mastery is reached within a particular vibratory range, that range becomes accessible at any time by that Soul. For example, when the Soul explores the fifth dimension, it designs fifth-dimensional forms to learn through, many of them, and they come and go, change shape and perceptions – you can say they "live and die". When the mastery of the fifth dimension is reached, that Soul has full unrestricted access to *any* format within that dimension – *it knows the Code of the fifth dimension*, and so it can manifest any shape or form it wants there (or it can leave that range altogether). The same can be applied to any dimension.

Inside our third dimension the Soul generates material bodies to learn through, and experiences life within this range. The body is designed specifically for each lifetime, and as learning progresses, the body experiences difficulties, struggles, joys, and it ages, then it dies. At that point the Soul designs another body, and so on (of course, it only looks linear from our third-dimensional perspective; in truth all these lifetimes occur simultaneously). When mastery of the third dimension is accomplished, the Soul gains unrestricted access to matter – *knowing the Code of this dimension* the Soul can maintain the body indefinitely, it can change the body's shape in any way it wants to (from tall to short, from a woman to a man, from a human to a lion, etc.) In other words, it can regenerate the material form indefinitely, making it basically immortal.

Our mission in life here inside matter is not to "escape this messed up world", or to be taken away from here by some external power (God, guides, ETs, the Soul, and the like) – it is to gain Mastery of the third dimension. Once that is achieved, we become enlightened (within an expanded range of perception), immortal (gain full access to the design codes) in the body, and we can remain here, or leave for the higher planes of existence and occasionally visit this one. It is completely up to us. But the goal is not to *leave*, it is to *gain mastery of this place.*

Immortality – the state of eternal presence – is not only achievable; it is a natural consequence of full awakening into Mastery.

But physical immortality is not possible without one's ability to vibrate at the fast frequency of Mastery. These are the components of this vibratory resonance:

- One must *want* to become immortal. The linear words are limited here, so it might be difficult to explain... This is not about the "fear of death," it cannot be, because if there is such a fear, it implies that one is still in the perception of separation, believing the idea that one might perish, and the material body is seen as a Self. Thus not fearing death, seeing it as a transition from one experience to another, is essential for the desire of immortality. It is not really about "immortality" anymore either, it is about expanding to such an extent that one *becomes pure consciousness*, which then can lovingly maintain the material body indefinitely (although there is *no attachment* to that particular shape and form!)

- Also, if life is difficult and dis-ease-ridden, one tends to desire an escape from matter, instead of living for thousands of years, which might seem more like a torture than pleasure, and so the desire is flat. This is also a limited perception issue, assuming that immortality means remaining in the same material form for eternity, limited by that form and by the laws of physics and time. <u>Immortality in its true form is an "access to the code of matter" which then can be used in any way we desire.</u> Imagination is a necessary component to opening up these perceptional limitations.

- One must believe that one does not have to die. This is a very difficult belief for most humans to let go of. Firstly, because there is proof of the "cycle of life and death" all around us, in Nature, and secondly, because human identity remains in the range of animalistic perception, or slightly higher, in the linear mind – still limited by the parameters of this simulation. Death is not the Law, it is pre-programmed code inside this simulation/reality. Once one's consciousness is *not attached* to Death or Life, one transcends the program of this simulated environment and it becomes natural to believe that one does not *have* to die. At that point Death is a *choice*, not the Law.

- One is required to release any separation and negativity that is stored within. One still experiences personal emotions, but all beliefs (which generate the thoughts, which then generate these emotions) are of an expanded nature, in alignment with the Divine Mind. Then any event is fully experienced on all levels, without any backlog or resistance, and learning is extracted in its entirety from every moment.

- One must become a Master of this dimension, which in its basic format means one must have full conscious command of one's physical, emotional, mental, and conceptual states at all times.

Cellular Longevity

Cellular regeneration (immortality) is dependent upon how much Mastery we have achieved. We are consciousness/energy inside a cellular system which is also consciousness/energy, but slowed down to such an extent, that it appears solid in this dimension. The original human design for this planet assured lifespans of thousands of years, learning something new with every cell's replication. This program is still encoded within our etheric bodies, but it does not run the material form anymore. Inside human DNA are components which correlate to different

174

frequencies, other than matter. They relate to the higher levels of the human energy system, mostly unexplored by current humans: the 9th – the Crystalline Unity Concepts, the 10th – the Support/Connectedness Experience, the 11th – the Akashic Memory/Archive, and the 12th – the Unity Consciousness Experience. The DNA code was designed to respond to material density, etheric density (1st), crystalline density (9th), and the Akashic density (11th). The more highly charged filaments have allowed for the active regeneration of physical DNA.

The etheric DNA range holds all of the information about our full potential, everything that we can be in the most balanced state. There are no codes for aging in this harmonious genetic blueprint. This component is capable of boundlessly learning and processing new input of information, and it holds a direct link to Source energy – the infinite supply for regeneration of the matter-vehicle.

You might be wondering, what stops regeneration? Basically – toxicity: toxic feeding, toxic feeling, toxic thinking, toxic believing, and so on. Toxicity becomes a state of being, programming the body. The endocrine glands, like the pituitary and pineal, respond to the program of toxicity instead of the code of Light, halting regeneration.

But here is a more complex answer. Cellular regeneration is stopped by two components, added into the original human design. One of them is a "compatibility adjustment" and the other is a "virus". The former is called "inhibitor" and the latter is called a "blocker".

In the original human design the processing of incoming experiential data was incomplete (because of overwhelm, pain and other difficulties encountered during learning), which created the *need* for the inhibitors. These inhibitors were installed into the

Crystalline templates (the part of the DNA that responds to the ninth level of the energy field), which interrupted the flow of the life force from the Soul through the Crystalline and Akashic templates into the etheric and physical DNA portions. This disrupted the DNA feeding cycle. The inhibitors limit the flow of energy that feeds the etheric component of our DNA, separating Conceptual, Crystalline and Akashic from the etheric and physical. This allowed for many of the etheric components to become dormant, which facilitated the transfer of energy feeding them into the physical components, nourishing them instead. Minimized charge available for regeneration generated more physical limitation, but in doing so, created a smoother learning within the third dimension.

Inhibitors affect all of our DNA parameters. Within the etheric range they transfer some of the energy down to the physical, and they modify the health blueprint. In the Conceptual range they affect our perceptions and processing inside the belief systems. Within the Crystalline range they connect to the Light Body sacred geometry, but limit regeneration. In the Akashic range they relate to the journey and personal essence "signature", how it affects our perception.

The presence of the inhibitors made humans more compatible with this dimension while learning to become the Masters of it. These inhibitors are installed into our material design before every incarnation by the Soul. They are very helpful to our learning during the lifetime because they help us process life at the appropriate speed. Their purpose is to limit regeneration to the frame of a current lesson. Without them we would always know who we are, and because of it would not be able to learn – it is a self-imposed limitation for the sake of learning inside the third dimension.

Just like if you want to play the game of chess, you would have to agree to move the pieces only according to the rules of the game. You are aware that it is only a game, and so you can simply take the King and Queen off the board and proclaim that you have won. Yet it only *looks* like you have won; you have not *played* the game, therefore you would not have learned the skill of this game. Hence the limitation of the rules of the chess game is self-imposed for the sake of playing the game.

The inhibitors are here because of our own design, and for our benefit. Once we do not resist life, do not fight with our lesson plan, move through the lessons, and achieve Mastery, some inhibitors are automatically released. Why only some? Because the inhibitors we *can* release are linked to the Soul Contract of our *lifetime*. One can finish one's Soul Contract during the lifetime and the inhibitors of that lifetime are released. But if the full third dimensional Mastery is not achieved, there are other issues which are still to be dealt with which were not included into that particular lifetime, and they still do require inhibitors. In this situation the material life of the body is prolonged, and the body is able to receive more Light during that lifetime. But even if significantly reduced, there still is some aging, and eventually the Soul must leave that body. Then the new Soul Contract is designed by the Soul, and so on.

Our goal as humans is to courageously face our lessons during the lifetime (no resistance to the Soul Contract) which allows our bodies to live in health and harmony for a very long time – the aging process is significantly slowed down, one remains active, vibrant, and clear. One can even de-age once the inhibitors are released!

All inhibitors can be released only when we have become the Masters of the material plane. Then the physical DNA codes for full regeneration become active and a body becomes immortal – able to regenerate indefinitely.

Blockers on the other hand are karmic constrictions, compacted overtime. They also disrupt the original DNA function, but they are placed there by us, not by the Soul. Blockers split our DNA into little malfunctioning pieces. This limits the functioning of the physical genes, thus wearing the body down. It is the "de-stranding" of the DNA that many people in the New Age community talk about (although there are many misconceptions about what that means exactly).

Blockers are encoded through long term difficult karma, caused by the chronic backlog of the unlearned lessons.

These are the steps in formation of the blockers:

- When we resist learning, we become dis-eased;
- This stuck-ness is a negative friction which generates the blocker code in our DNA;
- It becomes karmic;

- Next lifetime we incarnate with that blocker already inside our genetic blueprint.

When we are unconscious, we generate more and more of the backlog of karma. As we awaken, the speed of perception becomes faster and the backlog is unavoidable.

Dealing with the resistance to the effort of learning is a fundamental component of awakening.

Because blockers separate physical and etheric DNA codes, when they are released, the etheric and physical ranges reunite, feed each other, and regeneration takes place.

The aging process is a result of the inhibitors, as is the loss of memory of continuity of our lifetimes, but the fast aging and dis-ease that we experience on our planet currently is the result of the blockers.

In the material body the blockers have an effect of toxicity, and as was already mentioned, this means that the endocrine glands are programmed to age our cells over time, instead of regenerating them. Dis-ease and decay of the cellular structure result from that toxicity.

This Universe functions by the Law of Attraction. When one's system resonates with toxicity, it only attracts more toxicity, degenerating the body through reprograming the endocrine system ("virus" of the blockers). But if we resonate with (vibrate at the rate of) the pure energy of the Source (Light) as much as possible, the blockers dissolve and the endocrine glands begin to do their job according to the health blueprint we originally programmed into our Soul Contract.

Endocrine glands like the pituitary and pineal can produce life-sustaining and life-enhancing hormones only when they are in alignment with the Divine Hologram for the matter-body. Light transmutes anything that is not Light, maintaining perpetual regeneration. The more Light we can maintain in our system, the more youthful we will be.

By clearing resistance to being a spiritual adult, by taking responsibility not only for our actions, but also for our emotions, our thoughts, our beliefs, we begin walking the path of our Soul Contract – and in doing so we release the blockers. By facing the circumstances of our lives and learning through them, we dutifully study inside our material classroom, and eventually we release the inhibitors. As that begins to occur, one would remember more of one's spiritual journey beyond this lifetime – past, parallel, future lifetimes – because the identity of this lifetime expands to incorporate the larger Self of the Soul, the Divine Mind is activated and knowledge that is not linear becomes readily available.

Evolutionary Acceleration

The human race, Earth and the entire Solar System are in the process of evolutionary acceleration. Our life-wave has completed the process of involution, and now proceeds further into an expanded evolutionary state. Life-waves are the descent of Soul groups into density. There are many of these life-waves, some are much more advanced than ours, and others that are just beginning their involutionary journey.

As the Earth rotates on its own axis, and in relationship to all other members of this Solar System, it continuously rejuvenates its relationship with the overall cosmic environment. The material forms of stars and planets represent the anchor-vehicles, of the larger inhabiting consciousness, which remains multi-leveled and often also multi-dimensional. As the stellar bodies, and the Earth, move through space-time, they bring the momentum of this self-searching disharmonious level of human consciousness to an end.

What might be perceived of as a planetary crisis, is actually the darkness of the womb, preparing to birth new life and levels of consciousness. A fruit rots to reveal a new seed. The deterioration and decay (in ecological, social, financial and political arenas) are the signs of completion of this dualistic consciousness paradigm.

We then move onto the harmonious realized-self level of human consciousness, leaving the space open for others from the incoming life-waves after ours, to step into our current awareness level, instead of falling under the hypnotic spell of fear-based instinctual group behavior, or even worse, karmic overlays (inherited patterns from other lifetimes that create victim consciousness all over again).

This upward evolutionary movement between the levels of consciousness requires effort, a focused intention to remain aware and Self-responsible. Following this leads to Awakening the Harmony within.

For those interested in further study

Feel free to search through different topics on my website to find what you are seeking. If you desire private support, read about my sessions and Night Quads. If you are looking for some free help, you can watch my videos with information from my first book "Mission Alpha," which is a composite of over ten years of teaching, seminars and private work. There are also recorded classes you can download if you prefer information in the audio format. And, together with my business partner Isabelle Lambert, I co-lead spiritual pilgrimages to the sacred sites of the world.

www.eugeniaoganova.com

Counseling sessions:

For over twenty years now, using my ability to see and read energy, I have helped people figure out solutions to many of life's challenges. It is important to me to see you empowered and strong, and so I teach you how you can grab the tail of your destiny and ride it, how you can become everything you are meant to be. Sure there are blocks in the way and they need to be worked on, and your effort is required for that task, but the result of confidence and connection to your Soul is well worth the process.

Read more about private sessions with Eugenia:

www.eugeniaoganova.com/private_sessions.htm

Night Quads (Harmonizations):

With so much going on in your life, it might be hard to stay sane and balanced. Add the planetary and star influences to that, and your life can quickly turn into a survival struggle. If you are interested in being balanced, in repelling overwhelm and staying anchored in your Self, the Night Quad is for you. It is a download of energy which I set up for you to receive at night, meant to align you with the planet and support all of the work you are already doing to stay healthy, harmonious and happy.

Read more about a Night Quad and how to sign up:

www.eugeniaoganova.com/night_quad.htm

Personal Growth Workshops:

In our workshops the recorded space is encoded with the energy patterns of the teachings in addition to the words. When you download the recording, you will not only be listening to a wealth of information, but be experiencing different states of consciousness as well. This is meant to be supportive of your journey, a tool you can learn to use in your everyday life.

Spiritual Tours:

There are many sacred sites on Earth – these are the places where Spirit touches the planet in a very intense way. The Light/Word/Code is more readily experienced in these places, which is why people of ancient cultures used them for their ceremonies, built temples and altars on them. Traveling to such places allows one to experience the energy of Light/Word/Code directly, uniting with the planet and the Universe. Teachings provided on such tours guide one along that path.

Here is the list of recorded workshops and tours available:

www.energypulsesource.com/events.asp

www.eugeniaoganova.com

"Mission Alpha: The Wise and Passionate You"

This is a complete manual for your energy system, one that you would have wished you had when you were born!

It contains, <u>in detail</u> information about:

- the energy field
- chakras
- color and sound resonance
- the physical body as energy
- how illnesses are created and how you can heal yourself
- how to come into more conscious contact with your Soul-Self
- how to become an authentic and joyful individual
- how to be in control of your destiny
- how to courageously face your emotional pain
- how to develop balanced relationships
- how to confidently manifest through your intention
- how to become a purposeful creator of your life.

The struggle with our bodies, emotions, relationships, careers and the meaning of life, is simply about us not remembering how to "read the manual" of our systems. The manual teaches us how to function in the awakened state that we are truly meant to live in.

Studying the manual implies some effort – we have to learn a whole new way of interfacing with our own consciousness that no one has taught us about before. Yet this effort is well worth it. It helps us to consciously understand our internal workings, beginning with our energy systems and look deeply into the physical, psychological and spiritual components of our psyches so we can discern what is not working and why, and learn how to fix it. Studying how we are designed leads to purposeful living and satisfaction. Courage, power, fulfillment and even happiness are energy states and in this manual I teach how to experience these despite negative external circumstances. Once you begin to feel more powerful and confident, the external environment will change to align with your new Self. Each one of us already has the "equipment", we just have to learn to "read the manual" and use it correctly. We must change our internal set up from autopilot mode to a conscious mode. In *Mission Alpha* you will read about where these "switches" are located and how to turn your Real Self on.

The real magic of life is about how Reality shines through the Illusion; it is the process of awakening. Alignment with the Source, the power of true identity, the balance of energy systems and the health of our physical bodies, all become enhanced by the expansion of conscious focus. This is the *Mission Alpha*, the primary mission, of every spark of God – us.

Paperback, 312 pages. ISBN-13: 978-0-9793817-0-6

www.eugeniaoganova.com/mission_alpha.htm

www.amazon.com

About the Author

I was born in Russia and from my early years have been practicing consciousness expansion – awakening healing work (which in Russia is called *tselitel'stvo*, the "wholeness-making") within myself, and with the planet, people and animals. I was born with an awareness of my Soul's journey and a memory of where I came from prior to birth in this life. I could see and read energies that were invisible to those around me and this ability, coupled with an intense curiosity, fueled my search for spiritual answers and an ever-expanding comprehension of how life works, who we are, the meaning of our journey in matter and how to make that journey the most efficient.

I have always felt myself to be "on a mission" – a mission of enlightment – for myself, others, and the planet. My clairvoyant abilities allow me to have an intimate relationship with Earth, Galaxy, and Universe, which have never felt far away to me. Being able to perceive the multidimensionality of universal energy, I live in a perpetual experience of Source's Light/Code in every moment, parallel to regular life's circumstances, thoughts and feelings. The holographic nature of our reality was apparent to me from birth, and exploration of that hologram became my life's work.

In 1992, with determination and courage and without speaking a word of English, my family and I immigrated to the United States from Russia, after the collapse of the Soviet Union. As an immigrant my life was difficult, yet people in need of healing and answers were always finding their way to me. As time went by, I learned English and worked at many jobs. I have studied science, history, archeology and astronomy in Russia and in the U.S. and have a BFA degree from the Art Institute of Boston. I now live in Maine with my husband.

My life has been about inspiration, personal discovery and the healing, teaching, and creative work for the benefit of humanity. For over twenty years now, using my ability to see and read energy, I help people figure out solutions to many life's challenges. It is important to me to see you empowered and conscious, and so I teach how you can grab the tail of your destiny and ride it, how you can become everything you are meant to be. Sure there are blocks in the way and they need to be worked on, and your effort is required for that task, but the result of confidence and connection to your Soul and Source is well worth the effort.

I believe that Awakening comes from Personal Mastery. Conscious awareness of our emotions, thoughts, beliefs – all that comprises our personalities – is how we become spiritual Masters in welcoming the Soul into our physical bodies. As awakened beings we are truly free to create the life we desire, filled with Joy, Creative Inspiration, Peace and Love. All we have got to do is apply consistent conscious effort and an amazing magical life will be ours!

www.eugeniaoganova.com

21733973R00110

Made in the USA
Charleston, SC
30 August 2013